How Children and Adolescents View the World of Work

John H. Lewko, *Editor*
Laurentian University

NEW DIRECTIONS FOR CHILD DEVELOPMENT
WILLIAM DAMON, *Editor-in-Chief*
Clark University

Number 35, Spring 1987

Paperback sourcebooks in
The Jossey-Bass Social and Behavioral Sciences Series

Jossey-Bass Inc., Publishers
San Francisco • London

John H. Lewko (ed.).
How Children and Adolescents View the World of Work.
New Directions for Child Development, no. 35.
San Francisco: Jossey-Bass, 1987.

New Directions for Child Development
William Damon, *Editor-in-Chief*

New Directions for Child Development is published quarterly by
Jossey-Bass Inc., Publishers (publication number USPS 494-090).
Second-class postage paid at San Francisco, California, and at
additional mailing offices. POSTMASTER: Send address changes to
Jossey-Bass Inc., Publishers, 433 California Street, San Francisco,
California 94104.

Editorial correspondence should be sent to the Editor-in-Chief,
William Damon, Department of Psychology, Clark University,
Worcester, Massachusetts 01610.

Library of Congress Catalog Card Number LC 85-644581

International Standard Serial Number ISSN 0195-2269

International Standard Book Number ISBN 1-55542-972-6

Cover art by WILLI BAUM

Manufactured in the United States of America

Ordering Information

The paperback sourcebooks listed below are published quarterly and can be ordered either by subscription or single copy.

Subscriptions cost $52.00 per year for institutions, agencies, and libraries. Individuals can subscribe at the special rate of $39.00 per year *if payment is by personal check*. (Note that the full rate of $52.00 applies if payment is by institutional check, even if the subscription is designated for an individual.) Standing orders are accepted.

Single copies are available at $12.95 when payment accompanies order. (California, New Jersey, New York, and Washington, D.C., residents please include appropriate sales tax.) For billed orders, cost per copy is $12.95 plus postage and handling.

Substantial discounts are offered to organizations and individuals wishing to purchase bulk quantities of Jossey-Bass sourcebooks. Please inquire.

Please note that these prices are for the academic year 1986–1987 and are subject to change without notice. Also, some titles may be out of print and therefore not available for sale.

To ensure correct and prompt delivery, all orders must give either the *name of an individual* or an *official purchase order number*. Please submit your order as follows:

Subscriptions: specify series and year subscription is to begin.
Single Copies: specify sourcebook code (such as, CD1) and first two words of title.

Mail orders for United States and Possessions, Australia, New Zealand, Canada, Latin America, and Japan to:
Jossey-Bass Inc., Publishers
433 California Street
San Francisco, California 94104

Mail orders for all other parts of the world to:
Jossey-Bass Limited
28 Banner Street
London EC1Y 8QE

New Directions for Child Development Series
William Damon, *Editor-in-Chief*

CD1   *Social Cognition,* William Damon
CD2   *Moral Development,* William Damon
CD3   *Early Symbolization,* Howard Gardner, Dennie Wolf

CD4   *Social Interaction and Communication During Infancy,* Ina Ć. Užgiris
CD5   *Intellectual Development Beyond Childhood,* Deanna Kuhn
CD6   *Fact, Fiction, and Fantasy in Childhood,* Ellen Winner, Howard Gardner
CD7   *Clinical-Developmental Psychology,* Robert L. Selman, Regina Yando
CD8   *Anthropological Perspectives on Child Development,* Charles M. Super, Sara Harkness
CD9   *Children's Play,* Kenneth H. Rubin
CD10 *Children's Memory,* Marion Perlmutter
CD11 *Developmental Perspectives on Child Maltreatment,* Ross Rizley, Dante Cicchetti
CD12 *Cognitive Development,* Kurt W. Fischer
CD13 *Viewing Children Through Television,* Hope Kelly, Howard Gardner
CD14 *Children's Conceptions of Health, Illness, and Bodily Functions,* Roger Bibace, Mary E. Walsh
CD15 *Children's Conceptions of Spatial Relationships,* Robert Cohen
CD16 *Emotional Development,* Dante Cicchetti, Petra Hesse
CD17 *Developmental Approaches to Giftedness and Creativity,* David Henry Feldman
CD18 *Children's Planning Strategies,* David Forbes, Mark T. Greenberg
CD19 *Children and Divorce,* Lawrence A. Kurdek
CD20 *Child Development and International Development: Research-Policy Interfaces,* Daniel A. Wagner
CD21 *Levels and Transitions in Children's Development,* Kurt W. Fischer
CD22 *Adolescent Development in the Family,* Harold D. Grotevant, Catherine R. Cooper
CD23 *Children's Learning in the "Zone of Proximal Development,"* Barbara Rogoff, James V. Wertsch
CD24 *Children in Families Under Stress,* Anna-Beth Doyle, Dolores Gold, Debbie S. Moscowitz
CD25 *Analyzing Children's Play Dialogues,* Frank Kessel, Artin Göncü
CD26 *Childhood Depression,* Dante Cicchetti, Karen Schneider-Rosen
CD27 *The Development of Reading Skills,* Thomas H. Carr
CD28 *Children and Computers,* Elisa L. Klein
CD29 *Peer Conflict and Psychological Growth,* Marvin W. Berkowitz
CD30 *Identity in Adolescence: Processes and Contents,* Alan S. Waterman
CD31 *Temperament and Social Interaction in Infants and Children,* Jacqueline V. Lerner, Richard M. Lerner
CD32 *Early Experience and the Development of Competence,* William Fowler
CD33 *Children's Intellectual Rights,* David Moshman
CD34 *Maternal Depression and Infant Disturbance,* Edward Z. Tronick, Tiffany Field

Contents

Editor's Notes   1
John H. Lewko

1. Children and Adolescents Look at Their Parents' Jobs   3
Chaya S. Piotrkowski, Evan Stark
Parents are important sources of information for young people regarding
the occupational system and work-family conflict.

2. Children's and Adolescents' Views of the Work World in   21
Times of Economic Uncertainty
Katherine J. Pautler, John H. Lewko
Views of the work world held by children and adolescents can be negatively
affected by communitywide economic circumstances.

3. Adolescent Work Perception: A Developmental Approach   33
Nicholas R. Santilli, Hans G. Furth
Adolescent work perceptions of employment are differentially related to
logical reasoning.

4. Young People's Attitudes Toward New Technology: 51
Source and Structure
Glynis M. Breakwell, Christopher Fife-Schaw
The motivation toward mastery of new technology is predictive of work-
related actions.

5. The Family Economic Environment as a Context for Children's   69
Development
Dale Clark Farran, Lewis H. Margolis
The complexity of the family economic environment must be acknowl-
edged in studies on children and their concepts of work.

6. Concluding Comments   89
John H. Lewko
Additional directions for research on youth and the work world are discussed.

Index   93

Editor's Notes

At the core of the transition from childhood to adulthood for most young people is the successful movement into the labor force. Yet we know very little about the views young people hold regarding the work world and the way in which these views are shaped or how they influence behavior. The movement into the work world typically involves a series of decisions; while it is accepted that subjective experiences play a role in the decision-making process, there have been few objective examinations of these experiences (Bloom-Feshbach, Bloom-Feshbach, and Heller, 1982). The work of Greenberger and Steinberg (1986) provides valuable insights into the impact of teenage employment on adolescent development, but we are still very limited in our understanding of how young people experience and perceive the adult work world.

This volume presents information from recent empirical investigations that have focused on children, adolescents, and the work world. We begin with the study by Piotrkowski and Stark, which looks at the family in general and at parental work in particular as a context for learning about adult occupations and the effects of work on family life. The authors examine the extent to which parents transmit their feelings and ideas about their jobs to their children and adolescents. They also examine the degree to which these young people are perceiving and responding to this information.

In Chapter Two, Pautler and Lewko consider the impact that severe community economic disruption has on young people's views of the work world. The authors suggest that the pervasiveness of economic uncertainty can play a major role in shaping the outlook of children and adolescents.

Santilli and Furth, in Chapter Three, look at young people's understanding of work through their perceptions of employment and unemployment. Unique to this study is its developmental approach, which examines the relationship between the development of logical reasoning and changes in work perception.

Chapter Four analyzes adolescents' attitudes toward new technology. Breakwell and Fife-Schaw take us through a series of investigations designed to identify both the structure and the possible source of orientations toward new technology.

The fifth chapter, by Farran and Margolis, examines the family economic environment for sources of influence that investigators may not be acknowledging in their studies of children and work. The authors demonstrate the potential complexity of the environment by considering six different variables, and they provide brief case studies that illustrate the instability of that environment.

The concluding chapter summarizes the themes running through this sourcebook and discusses possible directions for future research.

John H. Lewko
Editor

References

Bloom-Feshbach, S., Bloom-Feshbach, J., and Heller, K. A. "Work, Family, and Children's Perceptions of the World." In S. B. Kamerman and C. D. Hayes (eds.), *Families That Work: Children in a Changing World*. Washington, D.C.: National Academy Press, 1982.

Greenberger, E., and Steinberg, L. *When Teenagers Work: The Psychological and Social Costs of Adolescent Employment*. New York: Basic Books, 1986.

John H. Lewko is associate professor of child development and director of the Centre for Research in Human Development, Laurentian University, Sudbury, Ontario, Canada.

While young people are fairly good predictors of their parents'
job satisfaction and working conditions, they do not know
more about mothers' than fathers' jobs, even though
mothers may talk more about their work.

Children and Adolescents Look at Their Parents' Jobs

Chaya S. Piotrkowski, Evan Stark

Increasingly, psychologists have come to recognize that children's ideas about the world may help to shape their social development. Conceptions of the occupational world begin to develop relatively early (Looft, 1971; DeFleur, 1963; Nelson, 1963; Cummings and Taebel, 1980; O'Bryant, Durrett, and Pennebaker, 1980), and the family constitutes one source of information about it. Parents' own work experiences may indirectly influence the socialization, values, and job relevant behaviors of their children. However, children can acquire occupational knowledge directly. As they listen to their parents talk about their jobs, as they see their parents come home tired after a hard day at work, as they spend time at parents' workplaces, they may develop feelings and ideas about work (Kohn, 1977; Piotrkowski, 1979; Piotrkowski and Katz, 1982). Yet little research has been conducted on children's conceptions of their parents' jobs, despite considerable research on children's occupational aspirations and attitudes. The study reported in this chapter addresses this issue by exploring what children think and feel about the work their parents do.

This report is part of a larger study funded by the W. T. Grant Foundation. We wish to thank Madeline Burbank, Shirby Strang, and Harriet Boxer for their help with data collection and data analysis.

J. H. Lewko (ed.). *How Children and Adolescents View the World of Work.*
New Directions for Child Development, no. 35. San Francisco: Jossey-Bass, Spring 1987.

Some indirect research evidence supports the idea that parental work constitutes a meaningful learning context for children. DeFleur (1963) found that children's first-hand experiences with jobs were a more effective source of information about occupations than other sources, such as the media. Dyer (1956, 1958) found significant associations between fathers' own satisfaction and their children's satisfaction with the fathers' jobs. Moreover, children had concrete ideas about the fathers' working conditions. Dyer concluded that there existed familial communication about fathers' jobs as well as consensus about them.

Personal experiences may also affect occupational aspirations. In a large sample of eleventh graders, Tittle (1981) found that students mentioned direct personal experience—including having family members in an occupation—as being most influential in their occupational plans. In fact, in a study based on interviews, Piotrkowski (1979) found that some adults remembered forming opinions about their parents' jobs in childhood, and they attributed decisions about their own occupational lives to these early impressions.

This chapter further explores young people's ideas about their parents' jobs. Underlying our study is the notion that parental work experiences constitute a learning context—a living laboratory—for children regarding the occupational world and the integration of work and family life (Piotrkowski, 1979).

Several broad propositions guided our analysis. In the light of Dyer's (1956) research, we proposed that parents transmit their feelings and ideas about their jobs to their children. Specifically, we predicted significant agreement between (1) reports of parents' work experience (subjective and objective) and their children's views of them and (2) between children's satisfaction with their parents' jobs and parents' own satisfaction.

We were also interested in learning about sources of information about parents' jobs. Because mothers generally play a larger role in families than fathers do, we predicted that children would perceive their mothers' jobs as having a more negative impact on their families than fathers' jobs.

Finally, consistent with the hypothesis that adverse occupational conditions can "spill over" to affect family life (Piotrkowski, 1979), we predicted that the extent of work-family conflict reported by children would be associated with adverse parental job conditions—both structural and psychosocial. Beyond performing initial tests of these propositions, our interest was in describing occupational factors that may influence children's ideas and in developing some questions for further research.

The analysis described in this chapter is based on data collected in 1983 as part of a larger study of the effects of parental occupational stress on family dynamics and children's mental health. This chapter constitutes one report that has emerged from the larger study. Since the data were not collected specifically for a study of children's conceptions of their parents' jobs, they have some notable limitations. First, the sample was not randomly selected, and socioeconomic status was intentionally restricted. Moreover, fathers' jobs were also limited by the sampling process. Consequently, any empirical generalizations drawn from the data analyses must be treated with caution. Second, the relatively small sample size, the broad age range of the children sampled, and the collection of data at one point in time did not permit a developmental approach to our analyses. Finally, because the exploratory analyses reported here are based on single items measured at one point in time, reliability was decreased.

Despite these significant limitations, the data have strengths that make them useful for an exploratory analysis. First, information was gathered from both employed parents and their children regarding the parents' jobs, enabling comparisons of the responses of parents and their children. Second, data were gathered about specific parental working conditions, so that analyses could extend beyond considerations such as maternal employment and socioeconomic status.

Overview of Study Procedures

Target Population. The focus of the larger study was on families of blue-collar, service, and nonprofessional white-collar workers. Restricting the population in this manner limits the generalizability of the findings (although, in fact, most adults work in such jobs). Narrowing the socioeconomic range of the population also limits variability, but it has the benefit of reducing the confounding effects of factors related to social class standing. Even within a limited socioeconomic range, there exists considerable variation in parents' actual work experiences.

The larger study focused on school-aged children for two reasons: First, they represent a population that has not often been studied. Second, school-aged children can provide relatively independent and reliable information. For the purposes of the analyses presented here, older school-aged children are especially appropriate because they already have developed a conception of work.

Sampling. Before we identified a sample of children and families, we developed a sample of occupations by identifying jobs within the target population that would vary according to the working conditions of interest. Three work sites in the Northeast were then located that would provide access to workers in such occupations—specifically, an aerospace factory, the postal service, and a small college campus. Data from questionnaires administered to more than 1,400 employees at these sites were used to develop population information and specific information about working conditions in a variety of jobs. Subsequently, a telephone and mail survey of more than 1,100 employees was conducted at those work sites to identify a sampling frame for the study of children and families. Because of an insufficient number of employed women with children aged seven through seventeen, employed women were not sampled further, and the college work site was eliminated.

The final sampling frame of eligible families for the larger study consisted of 188 families, most of whom were white. Only families with both parents present and at least one child between the ages of seven and seventeen living at home were included in the target sample. Fathers worked either at the aerospace factory or for the postal service. Up to two children in each family were designated as potential subjects. These children were selected by the research team to balance age and sex of child subjects. Children aged ten years and older were designated as "child-respondents" and were asked to provide information about themselves and their families. These child-respondents are the focus of this chapter.

Because of limitations in resources, data were collected through mailed questionnaires. Fathers reported about their jobs, marriages, and themselves. Mothers reported about their jobs (if employed), themselves, their marriages, and the mental health and father-child relationships of all subject children. Child-respondents provided information about themselves, their perceptions of their parents' jobs, their own occupational aspirations and values, and their relationship with each parent. Parents were given instructions about children's questionnaires, which were designed to be completed in two parts. Each child-respondent was provided with a sealed envelope for his or her questionnaire.

To encourage responses, the study team made multiple contacts with over 85 percent of the families. Families were paid $10 for participating, and children were given stickers as prizes. A family was counted as responding if at least two members completed the questionnaires and if information was provided about at least one child. Overall, eighty-three families responded, resulting in a family response rate of 44 percent.

The data analyses reported in this chapter are based on the eighty-two child-respondents (forty-one boys and forty-one girls) in the sample. Because siblings were included, these eighty-two children were members of sixty-four families. Of these families, forty-six (71.9 percent) had both an employed mother and father. A mother was counted as employed if she worked for pay, regardless of the number of hours worked. Thus, fifty-eight children lived in dual-earner households. Although all forty-six employed mothers returned their questionnaires, one child did not answer the questions about his mother's job. Consequently, we have paired child-mother data for fifty-seven of the children (thirty-one boys and twenty-six girls), with some instances of missing data on individual items. Of the fathers in these families, sixty-three returned questionnaires, giving paired father-child data for eighty children (forty-one boys and thirty-nine girls), with some missing data.

Measures. For the larger study of parents' jobs, scales were developed to measure five key job conditions: job control, job demands, job security, physical hazards, and relations with supervisors (Piotrkowski, Stark, and Burbank, 1983). These job conditions have been implicated in stress-related ailments for adults. For the purposes of this chapter, single items from these scales were selected for analysis. Employed parents also were asked about job satisfaction (two items) and work-family connections (two items).

The five job conditions of interest were used to guide the construction of items assessing children's views of parental working conditions. Children also were asked about sources of information on parents' jobs, their own satisfaction with each parent's job, and their ideas of parental job satisfaction and of work-family conflict. Most items were close-ended, and all items were piloted and revised. Questions about mothers' and fathers' jobs appeared in different parts of the questionnaire.

Self-administered questionnaires with children have not been established as a reliable method of data collection. Moreover, single items have relatively low reliability, and, in this case, test-retest data were not available. Nonetheless, there are indicators that children provided reliable and valid data: Few children had missing data; all the scales derived from children's reports in the larger study were internally consistent; and items measuring the same constructs in the analyses reported here were significantly and substantially correlated. Finally, in analyses conducted for the larger study, children reliably predicted parents' reports of family relationships.

Sample Characteristics

The average age of both the male and female child respondents was fourteen years, with a range of ten to seventeen years and no significant age difference between boys and girls. The eighty-two child-respondents included eighteen sibling pairs, of which four were same-sex siblings. In order to maintain sample size, we retained these sibling pairs for the analyses reported here.

The forty-five employed mothers for whom we have comparable data from child-respondents were on average in their early forties (M = 41.3, SD = 6.4). A majority had completed high school (86.7 percent), and 37.8 percent of the total (n = 17) had some level of postsecondary education. Comparable data from child-respondents are also available for sixty-three fathers, who were on average in their midforties (M = 44.3, SD = 7.3). Similar to the mothers, 90.6 percent of the fathers had completed high school, and 31.7 percent of the total fathers (n = 20) had obtained some level of postsecondary education.

Consistent with the demographics of the geographic area in which the study took place, families were predominantly Catholic. Forty-two percent of the fathers worked for the postal service (at a variety of locations), while the rest were employed at the aerospace factory. Fathers worked in eighteen different occupations in those two settings. Because all fathers were employed in unionized workplaces, wages were adequate and families in this study were not poor (average annual salary = $22,400; SD = 2,600). Fathers had been stably employed in their jobs for an average of twelve years (the range was from two to thirty-two years). At the time of the study, the forty-five employed mothers whose responses were analyzed had been in their jobs about five years on average (from under one year to thirty-one years). They worked from ten through forty-four hours per week: 13.3 percent worked fewer than twenty hours per week, 35.6 percent worked between twenty and twenty-nine hours per week, and 51.1 percent worked thirty or more hours per week. As expected, the older their youngest children were, the more hours mothers were employed ($p \leq 0.05$, one-tailed test). These mothers earned, on average, $7,900 per year ($SD$ = 4,600). Not surprisingly, dual-earner families had significantly higher household incomes than traditional families ($p \leq 0.001$), although the average difference was only $6,000.

Results

Simple group comparisons and correlations were the primary statistical procedures used, with both parametric and nonparametric techniques utilized (Siegel, 1956). One-tailed tests of significance were used only when testing directional hypotheses. Although the individual child was treated as the unit of analysis, the inclusion of siblings and parent-child pairings makes the data quasi-independent. The problem of nonindependence is minimized in the within-sex analyses.

There were few differences between boys and girls in the pattern of responses to mothers' and fathers' jobs. Unfortunately, given the small sample size, developmental trends could not be examined; however, we did consider the extent to which age might be related linearly to children's responses. Few significant associations with age emerged.

Sources of Knowledge About Parents' Jobs. How do children obtain information about what their parents' jobs are like? Data were available about two potential sources of information: visits to parents' workplaces and discussions with parents about their jobs.

Children were asked to respond to the question: "Have you ever visited the place your father (mother) works?" Responses could range on a three-point anchored scale from "never" to "many times." (No children circled "don't know.") Few children reported never having visited parents' workplaces. Children did, however, report visiting mothers' workplaces more often than those of fathers: Whereas 68.4 percent of the children reported visiting mothers' workplaces "many times," only 19.5 percent reported visiting fathers' workplaces "many times," a difference that was significant ($z = -4.38$, $p \leq 0.001$, two-tailed test Wilcoxon matched-pairs signed-ranks test).

The parental gender effect for visits to workplaces may be related to the limited paternal work settings sampled—one factory and the postal service. In contrast, mothers' jobs were unselected, and more variability existed in the settings in which they worked. It also is possible that the kind of work settings in which women often are employed more easily integrate children. Moreover, children on vacation are more likely to be with mothers at work than with fathers.

How frequently parents talk to children about their jobs, however, is not an artifact of the settings sampled. Yet results were similar for children's responses to the following question: "Does your father (mother) talk to you about his (her) job?" Responses could range on a three-point anchored scale from "never" to "often." Few children reported that parents never talked to them about work; however, significant parental gender effects were evident. Only 28 percent of the children reported that their fathers talked to them about their jobs often, whereas most children (52.7 percent) reported that their mothers did.

The parental gender effects for talking and visiting indicate that, in this sample, children had greater access to information about mothers' than fathers' jobs. If this is the case, we would also expect children to have more knowledge about their mothers' than their fathers' jobs. To examine this proposition, knowledge was considered from two perspectives: claimed knowledge and accuracy of knowledge.

Claimed Knowledge About Parents' Jobs. Children were asked to respond to a series of questions about specific parental job conditions. For example, they were asked: "Is it noisy where he (she) works." Children could circle "yes," "no," and "I don't know." To understand what children did and did not know about, patterns of "don't know" responses to nine of the items were analyzed. We were interested in discerning any reliable patterns in the child-respondents' claimed knowledge and in testing the hypothesis of a parental gender effect in extent of claimed knowledge or its absence.

The percentage of "don't know" responses varied considerably across the nine items, indicating children were discriminating in their responses. On the basis of these percentages, items tapping mothers' and fathers' job conditions were rank ordered separately. The two sets of rankings were very similar ($rho = 0.91$, $p \leq 0.01$), even when siblings were eliminated and ranks recalculated using two independent samples: children with employed mothers (for ranking mothers' job conditions) and children with nonemployed mothers (for ranking fathers' job conditions). In this sample at least, children's knowledge claims followed similar patterns regardless of whether women's or men's jobs were considered.

Because of the similarity in rankings, it becomes meaningful to determine the kinds of job conditions children claimed most and least knowledge about. Children claimed knowledge about job loss, the physical environment at work, and one job demand—working hard. They claimed less knowledge about job control, relations with supervisors, and the job demand of working fast. Thus, the more subtle aspects of the job—such as degree of task control and social relations—were more elusive than concrete physical conditions and a specific event such as job loss.

While the rank orders provide some information about similarities in patterns of claimed knowledge about men's and women's jobs over all children, they do not tell us if *levels* of claimed knowledge differed for mothers and fathers. To test the hypothesis that children claim more knowledge about their mothers' than their fathers' jobs, we created summary "don't know" scores for children in dual-earner families. Scores could range theoretically from 0 through 9. There were no sex differences in these scores and no significant linear relationship with age.

Children who claimed knowledge about their fathers' job conditions tended to claim knowledge about their mothers' working conditions ($r = 0.38$, $p \leq 0.01$). Consequently, a paired t-test was used to determine if mean "don't know" scores for mothers' and fathers' jobs differed. As predicted, children claimed significantly more knowledge about mothers' than fathers' jobs ($t(56) = 4.07$, $p \leq 0.001$). "Don't know" responses for fathers' jobs averaged 3 per child versus 1.7 per child for mothers' jobs.

Was claimed knowledge associated with the frequency of talks with parents about their jobs or visits to parents' places of work? To find out, we correlated summary "don't know" scores with reports of talking and visiting. All correlation coefficients for talking—but not for visiting—were significant, as predicted. The more children reported talking with a parent about his or her job, the lower his or her "don't know" score was (correlations ranged from $r = -0.34$ to -0.49). Fathers (but not mothers) also had been asked how frequently they spoke with their children about work. Fathers' reports of frequency of talking also were significantly correlated with children's claimed knowledge ($r = 0.31$ for both boys and girls). The more often fathers report talking, the lower their children's "don't know" scores were. Curiously, fathers' reports of the frequency with which they spoke with their children about the job were only marginally correlated with children's reports of how often their fathers talked ($r = 0.17$, $p \leq 0.07$, one-tailed test). Possibly, fathers and children have different conceptions of what it means to talk about the job, but in each case children believe that information is being transmitted.

Accuracy of Knowledge About Parents' Work Experiences. A major hypothesis of this study was that children have relatively accurate knowledge about parents' working conditions. This hypothesis was tested by comparing children's perceptions of parents' work experiences with reports provided by their parents. Two aspects of work-related experience were investigated: parents' subjective attitudes about the job (that is, their job satisfaction) and actual job conditions. Because mothers appeared to provide children with more information, the secondary hypothesis that children were more accurate reporters about their mothers' than their fathers' jobs also was considered.

Children's assessments of how satisfied they perceived their parents to be (1 item) were compared with parents' reports of their own satisfaction (2 items). In all cases, children's reports were significantly correlated with parents' reports as predicted (correlations ranged from $r = 0.37$, $p \leq 0.01$ to $r = 0.52$, $p \leq 0.001$). The pattern was similar when boys and girls were analyzed separately. Because single items have limited reliability, the strength and consistency of the other associations are all the more impressive. A nonsignificant correlation between children's predictions of their mothers' and their fathers' job satisfaction also indicates that children discriminated between parents. Children also predicted mothers' and fathers' job satisfaction with equal accuracy, a finding that is not consistent with the hypothesis that children are more knowledgeable about mothers' than fathers' subjective attitudes. However, the data may have provided an insufficient test of the hypothesis since mothers reported more satisfaction than fathers, and the range of their responses was thereby restricted.

A possible generalized family trait to report satisfaction—a sort of social desirability set at the level of families—was ruled out as accounting for the findings. Correlations between husbands' and wives' reports of job satisfaction were nonsignificant or negative. Correlations between children's assessments of one parent's job satisfaction and the actual satisfaction of the other parent also tended to be negative, contrary to what one would expect from a generalized social desirability set. Apparently, children do know something of how their parents feel about jobs.

Accuracy of knowledge about specific job conditions also was considered. Children who reported they did not know about a particular job condition were dropped from the analysis of the item. Using related items from the parents' and children's questionnaires, children were divided into two groups: those who said a particular job condition was present and those who said it was not. Parents' reports for the two groups were compared, using both parametric and nonparametric statistics as checks on each other. For these analyses, boys and girls were combined to maintain cell sizes. The results are listed in Table 1.

Results for fathers are relatively clear. Children who claimed knowledge about fathers' working conditions were able to reliably distinguish qualitative differences in fathers' reported working conditions. Regardless of the type of statistic computed and even with siblings removed, eight of eleven tests were significant.

Specifically, children were accurate about the physical environ-

Table 1. Children's Knowledge of Father's Job Conditions

	Children's Reports of Presence of Condition				
	"Yes"		"No"		
Fathers' Reports[a] of:	M	(SD)	M	(SD)	t
1. Working Fast	2.8	(0.9)	2.4	(1.2)	1.17
Working Hard	2.4	(0.9)	3.0	(0.9)	-1.67^c
2. Task Control	2.7	(1.0)	2.3	(0.8)	1.26
Organizing Work	2.4	(1.2)	2.4	(1.2)	0.05
Monotonous Work	2.4	(0.9)	2.9	(0.8)	-1.99^c
3. Hostile Super[b]	1.7	(0.8)	3.0	(0.7)	-4.29^d
Hostile Super[b]	2.8	(0.8)	2.1	(1.1)	1.93^c
4. Noise	2.4	(0.7)	1.5	(0.7)	3.65^d
Risks	2.2	(0.6)	1.6	(0.6)	3.78^d
Hazards	2.2	(0.7)	1.6	(0.8)	3.05^1
5. Feeling Secure	2.1	(1.1)	3.4	(1.0)	-4.65^d

[a] All response formats for fathers' reports are on a four-point scale, except for the physical environment items, which are on a three-point scale.
[b] One item asked children if supervisors were "mean." A second item asked if supervisors were "fair."
[c] $p \leq 0.05$ (All of these are one-tailed tests.)
[d] $p \leq 0.001$
[1] $p \leq 0.01$

ment—noise and dangers, fathers' experience with supervisors, job demands (that is, effort), and job insecurity. (Lack of variability regarding job loss did not allow statistical analysis for an item inquiring about layoff, as almost all children and fathers reported no job loss.) Job control and working fast, however, were more elusive. Possibly, these questions were too vague to be meaningful, or the working conditions were too abstract and little talked about. It should be noted, too, that these were job conditions about which many children claimed little knowledge.

The analysis for mothers' working conditions was less reliable because of small cell sizes and limited variability in responses. There was little variation in children's and mothers' reports about physical hazards (most agreed there were few), in reports about supervisors (most agreed there was little hostility or meanness), and in reports of job loss. Consequently, meaningful statistical analyses for these job conditions could not be made.

Using a cell size of $n \leq 5$ as a minimum, six group comparisons were made. As in the case of fathers, children reliably discriminated job-secure from job-insecure mothers ($t(48) = -7.31$, $p \leq 0.001$), monotony

($t(41)$ = –2.28, $p \leq 0.05$), and noisy environments ($t(48)$ = 2.7, $p \leq 0.01$). They did not reliably discriminate job control or job demands (working hard and fast). Thus, in some limited respects, results for mothers are similar to those for fathers.

Overall, the findings are consistent with the notion that children know something of their parents' actual work experiences. The findings do not support the hypothesis that children have more accurate knowledge about mothers' than about fathers' jobs. Greater variation in mothers' working conditions would allow a better test of this hypothesis.

Degree of Consensus About Parents' Job Satisfaction. Based on the proposition that parents and children communicate about parents' jobs, we also tested the prediction that there exists subjective consensus about parents' jobs (Dyer, 1958). Correlation coefficients were computed between children's reported satisfaction with their parents' jobs and two items measuring parents' satisfaction directly. (Neither child's age nor sex was correlated with their reported satisfaction.) Results weakly support the hypothesis that there is subjective consensus about job satisfaction. Results were most clear in the case of boys and mothers: the correlations between son's satisfaction with their mothers' jobs and mothers' own satisfaction were r = 0.46, $p \leq 0.01$; r = 0.53, $p \leq 0.01$.

These data are not robust enough to conduct meaningful path analyses, but future research might examine the various direct and indirect influences on children's satisfaction with parents' jobs. These include children's beliefs about parents' satisfaction, their perceptions of parental working conditions, and parents' own feelings of satisfaction.

Children's Views of Work-Family Conflicts. Children were asked to respond to the question: "Do you think your fathers' (mothers') job gets in the way of your family life?" Responses could range on a three-point anchored scale from "no, not at all" to "yes, a lot." (Only one child circled "don't know.") Parents were asked two questions: (1) "Have you experienced any family problems in the last month over your job?" Possible responses were "yes," "no," and "don't recall." (2) "In general, how does your job affect your family life?" Responses could range on a five-point anchored scale from "very negatively" to "very positively." In addition to testing the hypothesis that children report more interference from mothers' than from fathers' jobs, we also were interested in describing children's views of work-family conflict and in exploring determinants of children's ideas about interference.

Boys and girls did not differ significantly in the pattern of their responses regarding perceived interference from parents' jobs, but younger girls were more likely to report interference from fathers' jobs than older girls (r = –0.46, $p \leq 0.01$, two-tailed test). Children's reports of interference from their mothers' and fathers' jobs were not significantly correlated, indicating that they were making independent assessments.

The majority of children reported no interference from mothers' and fathers' jobs (59.6 percent and 72 percent, respectively). About one-third reported some interference from mothers' jobs, and about one-quarter reported some interference from fathers' jobs. To test the hypothesis that children experience significantly more interference from mothers' than from fathers' jobs, responses by children in dual-earner families were analyzed so that children could serve as their own controls. The Wilcoxon matched-pairs signed-ranks test was marginally significant in the direction predicted ($z = -1.59$, $p \leq 0.056$, one-tailed test), suggesting that children are more sensitive to interference from mothers' than fathers' jobs. This heightened sensitivity is further reflected in the finding that children's reports of interference were significantly related to mothers'—but not fathers'—reports of family problems resulting from their jobs. Employed mothers who indicated they had experienced a problem because of their jobs within the past month had children who reported more interference from mothers' jobs ($z = -3.45$, $p \leq 0.001$, one-tailed test). The effect held for both boys and girls.

A second hypothesis tested was that extent of work-family conflict reported by children is associated with adverse working conditions experienced by parents. Piotrkowski (1979) has hypothesized that numerous structural and psychosocial aspects of the job may interfere with the performance of family roles. Structural dimensions include time (for example, excessive working hours), timing of work hours (such as nonstandard shifts), and wages (specifically, unstable or inadequate income). Studies of adults—including the large job survey undertaken by us—indicate shift work to be a major contributor to reported work-family conflict (Staines and Pleck, 1983). Afternoon-evening work is a special problem for school-aged children because they may not see their parents when they come home from school and are asleep when their parents come home from work (Mott, Mann, McLoughlin, and Warwick, 1965; Piotrkowski and Gornick, in press). In this study, some data were available on shift work and hours, but the effects of low wages were not examined because the sample had been selected for generally adequate salaries.

Psychosocial factors that may increase interference include job stressors that induce psychological strain and inhibit positive participation in the family by increasing withdrawal or negative interactions (Piotrkowski, 1979). Job stressors measured here were excessive demands, poor relations with supervisors, job insecurity, and noxious physical conditions. Lack of job control also is a psychosocial stressor, whereas adequate control may reduce interference. Katz and Piotrkowski (1983) found that job control enhanced mothers' abilities to fulfill family role obligations, and Staines and Pleck (1983) found that scheduling control could reverse the negative effects of shift work on family participation. Thus, job control would be expected to reduce work-family conflict because it allows microadjustments in the complex transitions between work and home (Staines and Pleck, 1983). It was assumed that these effects of working conditions were potent enough to be seen in children's reports of work-induced interference. Exploratory tests of these hypotheses were conducted by computing correlation coefficients between parents' reports of their working conditions and sons' and daughters' reports of interference from parents' jobs.

Mothers and Work-Family Conflict. Traditionally, psychologists and sociologists have treated wives' absence from the family and the diminished mother-child contact resulting from employment as critical for families and children. In the context of the model described above, the structural variable of work time has been assumed to be especially salient in the case of women. In fact, when children in this sample were asked what they liked most and least about each parents' job, time and parent-child contact were mentioned frequently, in the case of *both* parents. Good hours and opportunities for contact were often listed as what they liked best, while poor schedules and insufficient contact with a parent was what they liked least. (These questions were open-ended.)

If maternal absence due to employment is problematic, it is reasonable to expect that more hours spent in employment result in greater reported interference. However, this hypothesis was not supported. For the combined group of children, more hours were associated with less reported interference ($r = -0.26$, $p \leq 0.03$, one-tailed test). This may be an artifact of the sample or a chance finding, but the finding suggests the possibility that women who work part-time do so partly *because* their work is viewed by family members—including children—as interfering with the life of the family. Full-time employment may occur more readily when all family members believe it is not a problem.

It should be noted that mothers in this sample did not tend to work excessive hours. The negative effects of employment hours on children and families may be apparent only under extreme conditions (Piotrkowski and Gornick, in press). However, shift work can be one such extreme condition, and the few mothers who worked a nonstandard shift had children who reported more interference, as predicted ($r = 0.27$, $p \leq 0.05$).

Because of limits in sample size and in the range of workplace variables measured—notably, physical hazards and hostility from supervisors—interpretation of results regarding psychosocial job stressors for mothers must be treated cautiously. Despite limited variability, mothers who worked in relatively more hazardous physical environments had sons who reported more interference ($r = 0.44$, $p \leq 0.008$ for both items). However, contrary to expectation, greater decision over job tasks (an aspect of job control) was related to *increased* reports of interference by daughters ($r = 0.39$, $p \leq 0.05$) and marginally by sons ($r = 0.25$, $p \leq 0.10$). These results raise the possibility that reports of such task latitude indirectly reflect work at home (such as giving piano lessons). This idea gains some

16

support from the fact that an item measuring mothers' ability to choose the hours they worked—often greatest when mothers worked at home—also was associated with increased reports of interference by daughters ($r = 0.39$, $p \leq 0.05$) and marginally by sons ($r = 0.34$, $p \leq 0.10$). Ironically, mothers may view at-home work as a way to minimize work-family conflict, while it actually creates difficulties for children. Perhaps having mothers at home—yet not having them accessible—heightens children's sense of deprivation. The increasing emphasis on new technology and at-home jobs for women makes it useful to explore these suggestions.

Fathers and Work-Family Conflict. Results for fathers and daughters most clearly fit the hypotheses. Eight of the thirteen correlation coefficients calculated were significant in the predicted direction (coefficients could not be calculated for hours fathers were employed because of little variation in this variable). Structural aspects of fathers' jobs contributed to reports of interference: girls reported more interference when fathers worked at a second job ($r = 0.33$) and when fathers worked a nonstandard shift ($r = 0.46$). Presumably, fathers' "moonlighting" (measured as a dichotomous variable) reflected the problem created by excessive working hours (boys also reported more interference from second jobs: $r = 0.56$, $p \leq 0.001$). As predicted, job control, as measured by two task latitude items ($r = -0.28$, $r = -0.34$) and lack of monotony ($r = 0.36$), decreased interference. Adverse psychosocial factors—job insecurity (feeling secure, $r = -0.60$; threat of layoff, $r = 0.61$) and noise ($r = 0.30$)—also contributed to work-family interference.

Fathers' job insecurity may be especially potent because it represents both a psychological stressor and a direct threat to the family's economic integrity. While boys and girls were equally knowledgeable about paternal job security, only girls' assessments of interference from work were correlated with girls' security ($r = -0.32$, $p \leq 0.05$). Perhaps girls are especially sensitive to the adverse family impact of potential job loss. Mothers' job insecurity had relatively negligible impacts. Perhaps it is less threatening to families because mothers usually earn less.

Directions for Future Research

Obviously, conclusions drawn from a small, nonrepresentative sample such as this are suspect until replicated by further research. Moreover, any generalizations must be limited to working-class, primarily white, young males and females. Still, the fact that findings were generally consistent with the research hypotheses lends some credibility to the results. Most important, perhaps, is that the results help us to think about the ways in which parents may contribute to children's learning about the occupational world, and they pose questions that suggest interesting directions for future research.

For example, we found that young people knew more about some aspects of parents' jobs than others. Relatively abstract aspects of the job—job control, in particular—were especially elusive. There may be a developmental progression in the acquisition of knowledge about occupational conditions, from the more concrete to the more abstract. Alternatively, parents may talk less about these more abstract job conditions and therefore hinder children's acquisition of knowledge about them. Research on the development of occupational knowledge in a variety of arenas—not just sex-role typing and prestige—would help address these alternatives. Also useful would be research that describes how and what parents talk about to their children and when they "talk about work."

As predicted, children reported more interference from mothers' than fathers' jobs. However, contrary to prevailing notions about maternal absence due to employment, mothers' working hours themselves did not predict reported interference. In fact, few job variables were related to children's reports of family interference from mothers' jobs. This may have been due to sampling and measurement problems, but it is also possible that women's traditional responsibility for the psychological well-being of the family results in their protecting their families from adverse job conditions. For example, there is evidence in other research that women compensate for time away from their children by increasing the quality of the time they do spend with them. These compensatory and protective coping mechanisms, when they can be used, may limit negative spillover from mothers' jobs. But, under some extreme conditions, such as shift work, compensatory mechanisms may have only limited effectiveness.

In contrast, daughters were especially sensitive to work-family conflict arising out of fathers' adverse working conditions—both psychosocial and structural. Men may have a more limited repertoire of coping behaviors that protect families from the long arm of the job. Future research might consider the relationship of work-related parental coping mechanisms in relation to children's experiences, as well as children's observational learning of these mechanisms (Piotrkowski, 1979).

But why would daughters exhibit special sensitivity to the effects of fathers' working conditions on families? Again, artifactual factors that account for this pattern cannot be ruled out. However, it also is possible that male and female children are differentially sensitive to family issues and dynamics, that they rely on different cues when making assessments of work-family conflict, and that they have different experiences in the family as a result of parental job strain. Both males and females were sensitive to obvious structural factors, such as shift work and second jobs. However, daughters may be more observant than sons about behavioral concomitants of psychosocial stressors affecting fathers and may be more aware of the larger family context. Preliminary analyses in the larger study suggest, too, that sons experience parents' adverse occupational conditions more directly—in their interactions with their parents. Ideally, these possibilities should be explored in samples utilizing opposite-sex sibling pairs.

Certainly, this study raises many more questions than it can answer. But it does point to the importance of the family as a learning context about occupations, and it indicates the importance of treating occupations as conceptually complex systems with multiple effects on children and families. A first task is to describe, in a much more extensive way than has been attempted here, what it is that parents teach children through the work experiences they bring home. The eventual task is to determine if the information children acquire in their families affects the decisions they make and the ways in which they eventually manage their own work and family lives.

References

Cummings, S., and Taebel, D. "Sexual Inequality and the Reproduction of Consciousness: An Analysis of Sex-Role Stereotyping Among Children." *Sex Roles,* 1980, *6,* 631–644.

DeFleur, M. L. "Children's Knowledge of Occupational Roles and Prestige: Preliminary Report." *Psychological Reports,* 1963, *13,* 760.

Dyer, W. G. "The Interlocking of Work and Family Social Systems Among Lower Occupational Families." *Social Forces,* 1956, *34,* 230–233.

Dyer, W. G. "Parental Influence on the Job Attitudes of Children from Two Occupational Strata." *Sociology and Social Research,* 1958, *42,* 203–206.

Katz, M. H., and Piotrkowski, C. S. "Correlates of Family Role Strain Among Employed Black Women." *Family Relations,* 1983, *32,* 331–339.

Kohn, M. L. *Class and Conformity: A Study in Values.* (2nd ed.) Chicago: University of Chicago Press, 1977.

Kunin, T. "The Construction of a New Type of Attitude Measure." *Personnel Psychology,* 1955, *8,* 65–78.

Looft, W. R. "Vocational Aspirations of Second-Grade Girls." *Psychological Reports,* 1971, *28,* 241–242.

Mott, P. E., Mann, F. C., McLoughlin, Q., and Warwick, D. P. *Shift Work: The Social, Psychological, and Physical Consequences.* Ann Arbor: University of Michigan Press, 1965.

Nelson, R. C. "Knowledge and Interests Concerning Sixteen Occupations Among Elementary and Secondary School Students." *Educational and Psychological Measurement,* 1963, *23,* 741–754.

O'Bryant, S. L., Durrett, M. E., and Pennebaker, J. W. "Sex Differences in Knowledge of Occupational Dimensions Across Four Age Levels." *Sex Roles,* 1980, *6,* 331–337.

Piotrkowski, C. S. *Work and the Family System.* New York: Macmillan, 1979.

Piotrkowski, C. S., and Gornick, L. "Effects of Work-Related Separations on Children and Families." In J. Bloom-Feshbach, S. Bloom-Feshbach, and Associates (eds.), *The Psychology of Separation and Loss.* San Francisco: Jossey-Bass, in press.

Piotrkowski, C. S., and Katz, M. H. "Indirect Socialization of Children: The Effect of Mother's Job on Academic Behavior." *Child Development,* 1982, *53,* 1520–1529.

Piotrkowski, C. S., Stark, E., and Burbank, M. "Young Women at Work: Implications for Individual and Family Functioning." *Occupational Health Nursing,* 1983, *31* (11), 24–29.

Siegel, S. *Nonparametric Statistics for the Behavioral Sciences.* New York: McGraw-Hill, 1956.

Staines, G. L., and Pleck, J. H. *The Impact of Work Schedules on the Family.* Ann Arbor, Mich.: Survey Research Center, 1983.

Tittle, C. K. *Careers and Family: Sex Roles and Adolescent Life Plans.* Beverly Hills, Calif.: Sage, 1981.

Chaya S. Piotrkowski is associate professor of psychology, St. John's University, Jamaica, New York.

Evan Stark is Henry Rutgers Research Fellow in Public Administration and Sociology at Rutgers University.

Communitywide economic conditions seem to exert a greater influence on children's and adolescents' views of the work world than do individual family circumstances.

Children's and Adolescents' Views of the Work World in Times of Economic Uncertainty

Katherine J. Pautler, John H. Lewko

Significant changes in the world economy in recent years have increased anxiety about job security and unemployment. The impact of these economic conditions, however, is not limited to adults. Children and adolescents do perceive and understand facets of the adult-oriented society in which they live, including such aspects as work, business, and institutions. Information generated by parents, peers, and the media about prevailing economic conditions begins to be integrated at an early age in the career decision-making process (O'Neil and others, 1980) and may well affect the general views that children and adolescents develop of their future place in the work force. The purpose of this chapter is to examine views of the work world held by children and adolescents who have experienced two types of adverse economic conditions: direct exposure to an unemployed father in the home; indirect exposure to the generally negative economic conditions of the entire community.

The importance of investigating children's perceptions of the adult work world was underscored in a recent review article on work, family,

J. H. Lewko (ed.). *How Children and Adolescents View the World of Work.*
New Directions for Child Development, no. 35. San Francisco: Jossey-Bass, Spring 1987.

and children's perceptions of the world (Bloom-Feshbach, Bloom-Feshbach, and Heller, 1982). Their review emphasized the influential role of subjective experience and individual interpretation in shaping children's views of the world. The article revealed how little is known about the impact of adverse economic conditions on the child's view of the world, and it underscored the need for investigations that are ecologically oriented and that respect the subjective views held by children and adolescents.

Limited data on views of work held by youth are available from a study conducted in Alberta, Canada, during 1979 when the economic climate in the province was still very positive. Using a seventy-five-item instrument designed to assess student attitudes toward work, Maguire, Romaniuk, and MacRury (1982) examined the views of 1,035 ninth- and twelfth-grade students in eight locations throughout the province. Results indicated that the students were generally supportive of the traditional work ethic, and views of the work world appeared to become more realistic the closer the entry into the world of work. Key sex differences were obvious on a number of work dimensions and pointed to the tendency of females to continue to ascribe to stereotypic types of jobs and job patterns.

Since children and youth are continually being exposed to economic uncertainty, we directed our study toward an examination of the views of the work world held by children and adolescents who had been living in a community in which significant and prolonged employment had been experienced in the months preceding the study. The availability of normative data on adolescent views of work derived in a positive economic climate (Maguire, Romaniuk, and MacRury, 1983) provided the opportunity to examine exposure to adverse economic circumstances both at the micro level, characterized by paternal unemployment, and at the macro level of the entire community being affected.

Method

Study Context. The study was conducted in the northeastern Ontario regional municipality of Sudbury. With a population of approximately 158,000, the municipality is both a primary resource town and a regional center, and it reflects a mixed metropolitan-urban character. The city of Sudbury, where the majority of business and service operations are located, serves as the focal point of the area. Although the area has a moderately diversified economic base, it is renowned as the nickel capital of the world. Historically, the economy of the area has followed the boom-bust cycle typical of primary resource communities: Prosperity is linked to international demand for minerals.

Our study was conducted in mid 1983, at the height of a nationwide economic recession. The area suffered in the wake of this recession, with an unemployment rate in excess of 30 percent (the highest for any city in

Canada) for more than six months. The situation was distinguished from previous "bust" periods by the initiation of the planned reduction of 4,500 permanent jobs in the mining sector over the remainder of the decade. A minimum of 9,000 persons would be displaced by the early retirements and permanent layoffs.

Subjects. Study participants were drawn from students in grades six, nine, and twelve attending fourteen elementary and four secondary schools in the regional municipality, which included the city proper and the surrounding smaller communities. School officials identified a cross section of rural and urban schools that they believed would reflect a range of experience in regard to the unemployment situation. All available students in the selected grades were targeted for participation; parental permission was solicited in sixteen of the eighteen schools. Parental permission was not required in two of the secondary schools due to their policy of informed consent by students.

A total of 1,235 subjects, including 369 sixth-grade students, 437 ninth-grade students, and 429 twelfth-grade students, participated in the study. Females numbered 555, and males numbered 607 across the three grades (uncoded sex, $n = 73$). The sample represented 44 percent of the accessible student population. Refusal rates for sixteen schools, based on the unreturned and returned parental permission forms, ranged from 20 percent to 54 percent. The fact that the data were collected near the end of the school year probably accounted for some of the refusals. In addition, absentees on testing day resulted in a loss of fifty subjects.

While the sample was nonrandom, socioeconomic and ethnic characteristics of the participants resembled those of the regional population. Based on paternal background information coded according to the Blishen Socioeconomic Index for Canadian Occupations (Blishen and McRoberts, 1976), 13.7 percent of the sample was upper class, 35.5 percent was middle class, 17.4 percent was lower class, and 16.1 percent of the sample could not be classified due to missing information. Of the 7.2 percent from female-headed single-parent families, 4.5 percent was upper class, 30.4 percent was middle class, and 21.3 percent was lower class (43.8 percent unclassified). Paternal ethnic origins revealed that 34.1 percent of the sample ($n = 1,145$) were of British extraction, 21.6 percent of French extraction, 21.5 percent of Western European extraction, 9.3 of Eastern European extraction, 4 percent of other extraction, and 9.6 percent of unknown extraction.

Independent Variable. The study focused on the effect of exposure to adverse economic conditions on views of the work world. Exposure was operationally defined in two ways: First, subjects were classified according to the parental employment record for the twelve months preceding data collection. A subject was classified as having been directly exposed if the father had been unemployed for any length of time during the stated period. A subject was classified as indirectly exposed if they had lived in the economically depressed community for more than six months prior to data collection and if the subject's father had been employed during the entire period. Of the total sample (n = 1,235), 426 subjects fell into the direct exposure category; 680 into the indirect exposure category; 129 subjects were left unclassified. For the most part, subjects in either of the two groups were from intact families; twelve subjects were from male-headed single-parent families. For those subjects in the directly exposed category, 50 percent had mothers who were then working, 39 percent had mothers who had worked previously, and 11 percent had mothers who had never worked. Maternal work status percentages for indirectly exposed subjects were slightly different, with some 54 percent having working mothers, 40 percent having mothers who had previously worked, and 6 percent having mothers who had never worked.

Second, exposure to unemployment was defined on a macro level. While subjects were either directly or indirectly exposed to unemployment, they were all exposed to the impact of the mining layoffs and the high levels of unemployment at the community level. By virtue of living in the community, subjects were exposed to a negative economic climate that may also have affected them. The entire sample could be compared to normative data on views of work that were developed within a positive economic climate.

The norms to which our data were compared are represented in the Attitudes Toward the World of Work Index and were developed on a representative sample of junior and senior high schools in the province of Alberta (Maguire, Romaniuk, and MacRury, 1983). These data were collected in the fall of 1981 and involved 231 schools and 18,691 males and females in grades nine through twelve. At the time the data were collected, the province of Alberta was still experiencing a very positive economic climate. Both the oil and agriculture sectors were strong, and unemployment was very low (4 to 5 percent). The outlook for the future, particularly with regard to the petroleum industry, was very positive, with continued expansion in oil exploration due to high world energy prices.

Instruments. Two instruments were used to collect data in this study. Because a key variable in the study included exposure of the subjects to unemployment for the period of May 1982 to May 1983, a parent information form was devised to obtain employment history and occupation of the parent or parents. This questionnaire was attached to the consent form sent home from the schools.

A second instrument consisted of the Attitudes Toward the World of Work Index. The index, developed by Maguire, Romaniuk, and MacRury (1982, 1983), is composed of fifteen subscales of five items each and is designed to capture children's perceptions and anticipations about the world of work. The scales cover a number of work dimensions (Cronbach's alpha values as reported by Maguire, Romaniuk, and MacRury, 1983, appear in parentheses): preparation by school (.342); interest and variability in jobs (.483); diligence (.544); laziness (.620); job security (.343); positive employer characteristics (.502); independence (.496); money (.425); ambition (.309); locus of control (.571); confidence in succeeding (.399); negative employer characteristics (.532); social relations (.584); attitudes toward unemployment (.611); and general attitudes toward earning a living (.330). Scale scores are compilations of opinions relative to these broad work areas. Each of the seventy-five items is rated in a five-point Likert scale, and values for each of the fifteen subscales ranges from 5 to 25. Due to a machine scoring error for the ambition subscale, we did not include it in this analysis.

Procedure. In order to gain direct access to a large number of schools as quickly as possible, we solicited assistance from a regionwide committee that had been organized to serve as an advisory group in dealing with the economic crisis. The committee consisted of representatives from labor, business, government, education, and the human services agencies. Formal support was obtained, and overtures were then made to the elementary and secondary school systems in the region.

Information on parental employment in the twelve months prior to the study was first obtained by having school officials assist in distributing the parent information form along with the subject consent form. Questionnaires were then assigned identification numbers, along with a detachable slip containing the names of the subjects for whom parental permission had been obtained. In classroom groups, subjects were identified by their name, given the questionnaire, and instructed to remove the name slip prior to completing the questionnaire. Items were read to all of the sixth-grade subjects.

Results

Direct Versus Indirect Exposure. The Attitudes Toward the World of Work subscales were analyzed in a number of ways. Correlations were first computed using exposure as a continuous variable. Significant but very low correlations (the highest being $r = 0.09$) emerged for four of the fourteen subscales, indicating no systematic relationship between length of time father was unemployed and subject's rating of the subscales. Analyses of variance were then computed, using grade, sex, and exposure, which was treated in two ways: first as a dichotomous variable (exposed versus unexposed); then as four levels of exposure (never unemployed; unemployed for one to six months; for seven to twelve months; for more than a year). Identical results were obtained using both approaches, and significant findings are reported for exposure as a dichotomous variable.

Since the focus of the study was the potential impact of adverse economic conditions, only significant exposure effects are addressed. Age and sex effects are reported in Pautler and Lewko (1985). Only one significant exposure main effect and two exposure interaction effects emerged, suggesting that direct exposure to adverse economic circumstances through paternal unemployment, while present, did not have an overwhelming influence on children's views of the work world.

The main effect was observed on the positive-employer-characteristics subscale ($F(1, 1,029) = 3.856, p < 0.05$). While directly exposed subjects were less likely to evaluate employers as honest and fair, neither group held extremely strong views.

Two significant Exposure × Grade interaction effects were observed for the subscales of independence ($F(2, 1,029) = 3.8, p < 0.023$) and locus of control ($F(2, 1,029) = 3.67, p < 0.026$). The independence subscale rates the degree to which subjects value the preservation of their own independence above that of other job characteristics. Directly exposed sixth- and twelfth-grade subjects were more willing to sacrifice their independence at work than were their indirectly exposed counterparts, while the opposite was true for the ninth-grade subjects. With the child's transition into high school, perhaps the unemployment experience in the family increased the salience of school for the exposed ninth-grade subjects, since this is a time for major decisions regarding curriculum choice and other changes that directly involve the parents and that hold implications for the child's eventual occupational success.

The locus-of-control subscale measures the degree to which getting a job is seen as a matter beyond personal control or one of luck. While most of the subjects became more external with age and viewed getting a job as due more to chance or whom you know, the closer they moved toward leaving school, the Exposure × Grade interaction revealed that the sixth-grade directly exposed subjects were significantly more external in their views of getting and holding a job than were the sixth-grade indirectly exposed subjects, who were the most internal of all groups. Therefore, exposure to an unemployed father in preadolescence impacts on a dimension that has been linked to inability to succeed in obtaining work (Becker and Hills, 1981), and the exposure appears to launch these young males and females on an accelerated path in developing the view that obtaining jobs is beyond their personal control.

Negative Versus Positive Economic Climate. Availability of group percentile norms for the work index permitted comparisons of the subscale data for the ninth- and twelfth-grade subjects. Subscale mean scores were converted to percentile ranks, and tests for the significance between two proportions were then conducted, using the percentile ranks and the group norms. Table 1 presents the percentile ranks by grade and sex for the subjects exposed to the negative economic climate. The ranks were obtained

Table 1. Percentile Rankings[a] of Adolescent Subjects for Attitudes
Toward the World of Work Subscales

| Subscales | Pecentile Ranks | | | |
| | Males | | Females | |
	Grade 9	Grade 12	Grade 9	Grade 12
Preparation	45	56	39[b]	53
Interest and Variability	50	30[b]	34[b]	25[b]
Diligence	38[b]	44	28[b]	38[b]
Laziness	63[b]	62[b]	61[b]	57
Job Security	77[b]	67[b]	80[b]	71[b]
Positive Employer Characteristics	42[b]	44	20[b]	45
Independence	65[b]	56	56	41[b]
Money	28[b]	39[b]	41[b]	35[b]
Locus of Control	78[b]	81[b]	69[b]	90[b]
Confidence	15[b]	14[b]	06[b]	11[b]
Negative Employer Characteristics	64[b]	66[b]	58	49
Social Relations	52	56	32[b]	33[b]
Attitudes Toward Unemployment	28[b]	32[b]	25[b]	25[b]
General Attitudes Toward Earning a Living	42[b]	49	33[b]	28[b]

[a] Percentile position of group means for the exposed group in terms of the normative sample.
[b] Test for proportions significant at 0.01 level.

by comparing the mean scores of the respondent groups to the mean values on the appropriate normative table and locating the corresponding percentile rank.

Examination of Table 1 reveals that, of the fifty-six comparisons, forty-one were significant at the 0.01 level. On five of the fourteen subscales, the negative economic climate group was significantly different from the positive economic climate group across both grade and sex. On an additional four subscales, three of the four age-sex groups were significantly different from the normative group data.

Striking results were evident for a number of subscales. Views of employers appeared to differ as a result of the type of economic environment. The average exposed subject had lower ratings on positive employer characteristics, meaning that he or she was less likely to see employers as fair, honest, and upstanding persons than the unexposed subject. This negativity was especially pronounced in the exposed ninth-grade females. Attitudes about negative employer characteristics were higher among the exposed males. In these cases, employers were thought to be mostly concerned with looking out for their own interests.

Opinions regarding job characteristics also registered some change in response to the negative economic environment. Exposed subjects in general placed greater value on job security than on other job characteristics; were less concerned with seeking jobs that are interesting, challenging, and varied; and tended to deemphasize salary as one of the most important determinants of a good job. Exposed twelfth-grade females departed from their male counterparts in placing less emphasis on preservation of their autonomy, while the opposite was true for the exposed ninth-grade males. Both ninth- and twelfth-grade and exposed females differed from the exposed males and the unexposed groups in not viewing social relations as being an important determiner of job satisfaction. They were much less likely to prefer working with people and being part of a team.

Views about diligence, laziness, and unemployment provided some perspective about the work ethic espoused by the subjects. Exposed subjects, especially the females, held somewhat more negative views toward working hard regardless of supervision. Both exposed sexes were also somewhat more likely to go along with the idea of getting something for as little effort as possible and with viewing unemployment as less shameful and undesirable than the unexposed subjects.

Responses to the remaining subscales echoed the general pattern of exposure to a negative economic environment on views of the work world. The older exposed adolescents were less positive about earning their own way than were their unexposed counterparts. Confidence in their ability to get a job and to be successful was critically low in the exposed subjects, and they also saw getting and holding a job to be much more beyond personal control than did the unexposed subjects, with the older exposed subjects having a more external locus of control than the younger exposed subjects.

Discussion

What emerged from these data, particularly in the macro comparisons, was the pervasive effect of negative economic conditions on attitudes toward the world of work. Contrary to the findings reported by Maguire, Romaniuk, and MacRury (1982), in which adolescents subscribed to the traditional work ethic, subjects exposed to negative economic conditions in their community held a relatively jaundiced view of the work world. Furth's (1980) developmental model of societal understanding would place most of our subjects at the concrete systemic stage, suggesting that their views of the work world were reality oriented and would therefore enter into the processing of future experiences in the work world.

If, in fact, our subjects are operating on a conceptual understanding of the work world that is reflected in their responses on the work subscales, then an examination of the general pattern of these responses is in order. From Table 1 we can see that the subjects exposed to a negative economic community held views of the work world that would, at best, render their transition from school to work problematic. One cluster of subscales— laziness, diligence, and attitudes toward unemployment—could be inter- preted as reflecting upon their work ethic. In general, all subjects held views that suggested a shift in their thinking toward avoiding hard work, trying to get as much as possible without expending any effort, and dimin- ishing the importance of having a job. Feather and O'Brien (in press) reported three similar areas as being present in their sample of high school seniors prior to leaving school; their study differentiated between graduates who found work and those who became unemployed. The fact that our entire sample held such views of work would suggest that a larger number than expected could be at risk for experiencing unemployment upon exit- ing school, unless their views of work are modified in the interim.

A second cluster of subscales on which adolescents in the negative economic community held significantly different views from the norms involved interest and variability, job security, and money. Together, these subscales reflect a viewpoint of setting aside the dream of affluence in favor of predictability. It would be better to have a job than to be con- cerned about how much money it paid. Furthermore, it would be better to focus on a job with long-term stability rather than on one that would be interesting and challenging and that might be intrinsically rewarding. Such an outlook could be viewed as conservative in nature were it the only set of subscales on which the exposed subjects differed from the norms. However, when combined with the previous set, these results begin to suggest that the exposed subjects are becoming low risk takers who are unprepared to work hard. Such a combination runs contrary to the emerg- ing views of the labor market that suggest that young people must be prepared to work hard and to move between several jobs on entry to the work force (Reich, 1983).

A third set of subscales that were rated differently by the exposed subjects reinforces the negative impact that the community economic situ- ation had on the adolescents' views of work. The locus-of-control and the confidence subscales demonstrated the most extreme differences between the two groups. The adolescents who were living in the economically depressed community had very little confidence in their ability to get a job in the future and to be successful, even though virtually all subjects had indicated they were planning on leaving the community to look for work. The adolescents also held the view that getting and holding a job would be largely outside of their control. The sixth-grade males whose fathers were unemployed also held very strong external views.

Locus of control, as presented in the work index, is directed prima- rily to the belief in being able to influence the job process. While it may be argued that the extremely external view taken by the exposed subjects is an accurate reflection of the youth labor market, once again we must consider the subscale in conjunction with the others. When locus of control and confidence are joined with the previous two clusters, the full effect of the negative economic conditions in the community is realized. Now we have adolescents who appear as low risk takers who are not prepared to work hard and who do not believe they are capable of getting a job. This scenario parallels the growing literature on youth unemployment and its psychological effects (Furnham, 1985). If our adolescents maintain their current views of the work world, it is reasonable to expect some of them to experience such difficulties as increased anxiety and depression, poorer subjective well-being, and lowered self-esteem.

It must also be remembered that the career decision-making process is active during middle childhood and adolescence. In their study of high school seniors and university students, O'Neil and others (1980) found that 84 percent of the subjects perceived that the "individual" factor, which was comprised of self-expectancies, abilities, interests, and achievement needs, affected their career decision making significantly more than external factors such as family, peers, or school. Since emerging views of the work world are essentially an individual process, we can assume that such views will enter into the career decisions of adolescents. How such views might shape the decisions is not known; however, it is clear that young individuals engaged in this process who are living in a community characterized by adverse economic circumstances could be viewed as disadvantaged.

In concluding this examination of our data on children's and adolescents' views of the work world, we think it may be profitable to place such views within the context of portrayals of the work environment of the future. These portrayals suggest that workers will need to be relatively autonomous, internally motivated, and, perhaps most important, keyed to the need for flexibility and adaptability (Butler, 1984). If the work subscales are evaluated for indications of flexibility and adaptability, the following pattern emerges: flexibility—high on interest and variability, independence, confidence, and internal on locus of control; inflexibility—low on job security, and viewing unemployment as undesirable. It is evident that the views of the work world held by the current sample of children and adolescents run contrary to the notion of their evolving as flexible and adaptable workers. This discrepancy points to an urgent need for research on how the emerging views of work held by young people affect their actual work choices and behavior.

References

Becker, B. E., and Hills, S. M. "Youth Attitudes and Adult Labor Market Activity." *Industrial Relations*, 1981, *20*, 60–69.
Blishen, B. R., and McRoberts, H. A. "A Revised Socioeconomic Index for Occupations in Canada." *Review of Canadian Sociology and Anthropology*, 1976, *13*, 71–80.

Bloom-Feshbach, S., Bloom-Feshbach, J., and Heller, K. A. "Work, Family, and Children's Perceptions of the World." In S. B. Kamerman and C. D. Hayes (eds.), *Families That Work: Children in a Changing World.* Washington, D.C.: National Academy Press, 1982.

Butler, D. *Futurework.* New York: Holt, Rinehart & Winston, 1984.

Feather, N. T., and O'Brien, G. E. "A Longitudinal Study of the Effects of Employment and Unemployment on School Leavers." *Journal of Occupational Psychology,* in press.

Furnham, A. "Youth Unemployment: A Review of the Literature." *Journal of Adolescence,* 1985, *8,* 109–124.

Furth, H. G. *The World of Grown-Ups: Children's Conceptions of Society.* New York: Elsevier, 1980.

Maguire, T., Romaniuk, E., and MacRury, K. "Opinions of Alberta Students Toward Work." *Alberta Journal of Educational Research,* 1982, *28,* 226–247.

Maguire, T., Romaniuk, E., and MacRury, K. *Attitudes Toward the World of Work: Development of the Scales and Manual for Administration, Scoring, and Interpretation.* Edmonton, Alberta, Canada: Planning Services Branch, Alberta Education, 1983.

O'Neil, J. M., Ohlde, C., Tollefson, N., Barke, C., Piggott, T., and Watts, D. "Factors, Correlates, and Problem Areas Affecting Career Decision Making of a Cross-Sectional Sample of Students." *Journal of Counseling Psychology,* 1980, *27,* 571–580.

Pautler, K. J., and Lewko, J. H. "Student Opinions of Work in Positive and Negative Economic Climates." *The Alberta Journal of Educational Research,* 1985, *31,* 201–208.

Reich, R. B. *The Next American Frontier.* New York: Times Books, 1983.

Katherine J. Pautler is a doctoral student in the Center for the Study of Youth Development, Catholic University of America, Washington, D.C.

John H. Lewko is associate professor of child development and director of the Centre for Research in Human Development, Laurentian University, Sudbury, Ontario, Canada.

During adolescence, significant strides in social understanding are achieved, particularly in the area of work perception, but what factors underlie this development?

Adolescent Work Perception: A Developmental Approach

Nicholas R. Santilli, Hans G. Furth

Contemporary scholars justifiably consider the development of a work orientation as a step in the adolescent's transition to adulthood. During this transitional phase, adolescents' relations to society's institutions change, as do their perceptions and understanding of these institutions. This chapter presents a developmental analysis of the changes in adolescents' perceptions and understanding of work as revealed by their concepts of employment and unemployment.

Recent investigations in the area of adolescent work orientation have focused either on personality variables associated with work, such as occupational identity and self-concept, or on the influence of working or not working on various developmental and behavioral outcomes, such as adolescent egocentrism, alcohol and drug abuse, or time spent with parents and peers (Hamilton and Crouter, 1980; Steinberg, Greenberger, Jacobi, and Garduque, 1981). Critics of these approaches suggest that much of the work orientation literature consists of an accumulation of research without a clear developmental perspective (Vondracek and Lerner, 1982). Their claim is that many developmental theories of career and work orientation are stage models that describe changes in work orientation as a function of age but do not adequately describe the process of stage transition within the context of existing developmental theories. In other words, the focus

J. H. Lewko (ed.). *How Children and Adolescents View the World of Work.*
New Directions for Child Development, no. 35. San Francisco: Jossey-Bass, Spring 1987.

has been on age-related changes in personality characteristics (namely, self-concept) correlated with work behaviors rather than on the development of adolescents' perception and understanding of work as a social institution. In addition, adolescent work experience in the form of paid employment is frequently an independent rather than a dependent variable. Thus, a significant portion of the adolescent employment literature describes the impact of part-time work experiences on outcomes other than work itself, such as educational achievement.

It should be noted, however, that these approaches to the study of adolescent work orientation have also made important contributions, extending the knowledge base in such areas as normative adolescent life experiences. Instead of abandoning current models of vocational socialization, we suggest that measuring what adolescents know and understand about work from a developmental perspective may contribute substantially to these very models.

Work Perception from a Developmental Perspective

Recent applications of a relational-developmental perspective in the area of social understanding provide a viable conceptual foundation for the study of adolescent work perception (Youniss and Smollar, 1985). The relational-developmental approach suggests that self-understanding and social knowledge are not acquired through self-reflection or imitation of social experience but are constructed through direct interaction between adolescents and representatives of society's institutions—namely, parents, peers, employers, and teachers.

Historically, adolescence has been perceived as a transitional phase unifying childhood and adulthood within the life course. As adolescents mature, they gradually acquire the privileges and responsibilities accorded adult members of society; these, in turn, expand the adolescent's societal experiences, providing them with a broader range of potential socializing influences, which then contribute to a richer understanding of personal and societal roles and functions. Social knowledge, then, is actively pursued within the context of mutual social interactions regulated by the standard conventions of social discourse—that is, by discussion, debate, and consensual validation of social experience.

Correlated with adolescents' increasing social participation is their personal intellectual development in the form of emerging logical reasoning capacities. The role of intellectual development in the construction of social knowledge has been a source of considerable debate. Recent reviews (Meacham and Santilli, 1981) have suggested either that cognition and socialization are parallel but independent processes, each progressing at their own rate and seldom interacting, or that cognition directly influences socialization through mediation of social experiences as a function of cognitive development—that is, of concrete or formal operations.

From the relational-developmental perspective, neither view adequately describes the nature of the cognition-socialization interaction. To claim that no relationship exists between cognition and socialization invalidates a large body of research in the area of social cognitive development. The problem must lie, then, with the relative influence of cognition on the acquisition of social concepts. Present models of social cognition consider logical reasoning to be at the core of socialization, in that cognition provides a necessary but not sufficient component to social understanding (Kohlberg, 1976). This view places cognition prior to social understanding; in other words, a prerequisite level of cognitive development must be attained prior to the acquisition of social understanding.

The relational-developmental perspective provides a third alternative to the question of social understanding. Instead of placing cognition in a mediational or prerequisite role, this perspective considers cognition as one aspect of general personal development that facilitates and is facilitated by direct social experiences. Cognitive development, then, does not control the acquisition of social knowledge in terms of being necessary for social understanding, but it provides a useful framework for interpreting and organizing social reality. Moreover, cognitive development does not proceed independently of social experience but progresses as a function of the successive coordinations of personal knowledge with changing social reality.

A relational-developmental perspective on work perception, then, would describe the growth in understanding of work-related concepts relative to personal intellectual development and expanding social experiences in the form of home, school, and workplace activities. This approach implies the synthesis of two apparently distinct forms of work perception—namely, a "subjective" understanding of *what* is known about work relative to personal intellectual development and an "objective," experiential view of *how* work concepts are construed within the context of interpersonal relationships.

In reality, these two instruments of socialization function in a complementary fashion, each facilitating and being facilitated by general social experience. Unfortunately, the interdependent nature of these processes complicates the study of work perception. Specifically, at what point does the analysis begin—at the level of *how* interpersonal relationships contribute to work perception or at the level of *what* knowledge and understanding adolescents possess about work? Furth (1978) has provided some guidance regarding this question: "The 'how' question [of objective social experience] is, however, premature until the 'what' question [of subjective social understanding] has been sufficiently clarified; that is, what knowledge or understanding do children and adolescents have of their society?" (p. 232).

To demonstrate this point, Furth (1980) interviewed children between the ages of five and eleven to determine their understanding of marketplace transactions, community relations, and personal and social roles. The most striking aspect of the results was the general qualitative transformations in these children's perceptions of society. Four levels of societal understanding were identified, each representing the genesis of societal concepts from childhood through preadolescence. The processes underlying the development of these societal concepts were the child's expanding social experiences and growing capacity to interpret these experiences. In particular, younger children demonstrated more personalized views of social reality corresponding with their limited social experiences and underdeveloped intellectual capacities. More elaborate perceptions of social understanding, characteristic of older children's views, were achieved in the context of personal intellectual development and increased participation in social institutions in the form of schools, peers, and community relations.

A Study of Work Perception

A relational-developmental approach is, thus, a fruitful point of departure for the examination of adolescents' knowledge and understanding of work. The focus of the present study, therefore, is on adolescents' knowledge and understanding of work relative to employment and unemployment, with an emphasis on the reciprocal contributions of personal intellectual development associated with general age differences in societal understanding.

Measuring Work Perception. Our sample consisted of 120 boys and 120 girls between the ages of twelve and eighteen from working- and middle-class backgrounds.

A survey of the adult literature provided an ample supply of potential areas of investigation. For this study, ten dimensions of work, five relating to employment and five relating to unemployment, were selected. A twenty-three-item paper-and-pencil questionnaire was developed covering these ten dimensions of adult work. A detailed description of this measure has been provided elsewhere (Santilli, 1985).

Of particular interest regarding the present study are nine items designed to allow adolescents to provide descriptions and explanations of their perceptions of employment and unemployment. Four items assessed knowledge of the employment dimension: (1) perceptions of worker qualities and (2-4) comprehension of the concepts of "work," "career," and "occupation," from a personal viewpoint.

Five items were constructed to ascertain adolescents' perception of unemployment: (1-2) the causes of unemployment, including both general and personal causes; (3) effects of unemployment; (4) forms of helping unemployed persons; and (5) the perception of society's view of unemployment.

Two measures of logical reasoning were also included to obtain a global estimate of intellectual development. A composite reasoning score was derived from these two sets of logical reasoning tasks as the criteria for placement into one of three reasoning levels: low (level 1), middle (level 2), and high (level 3).

Adolescents' Perceptions of Employment. Adolescents' descriptions and explanations of employment and unemployment were categorized using two criteria. The content of the descriptions was analyzed to determine the general knowledge adolescents possess about a specific dimension of employment or unemployment. This procedure focused exclusively on *what* knowledge adolescents demonstrated relative to work perception.

The analysis of adolescents' explanations of these same phenomena focused primarily on the depth of understanding associated with these descriptions and provided insight regarding developmental changes in societal knowledge.

Although effects due to sex and social class were also analyzed, it is beyond the scope of this chapter to present these results.

Perceptions of Worker Qualities. A genuine concern of every employer is choosing workers that possess the necessary qualities for optimal job performance. To determine if adolescents were knowledgeable of preferred worker qualities from an employer's perspective, we solicited descriptions and explanations of worker qualities in relation to work performance. Forty-two percent of the adolescents described specific occupational skills necessary for good job performance—namely, past work experience, necessary work skills, or appropriate training. Thirty-six percent described workers in terms of general personal traits amenable to the work environment, such as cooperative, trustworthy, or friendly. A substantial number (22 percent) provided descriptions of both the general personal traits and specific occupational skills necessary for optimal job performance.

Descriptions of worker qualities provided by twelve-year-olds focused primarily on the prerequisite occupational skills necessary for job performance, while fifteen- and eighteen-year-old students indicated a preference for personal traits associated with employment. The gradual transformation of these descriptions from external characteristics of occupational performance to internal, psychological traits correlated with work parallels a similar trend in descriptions of poverty and social inequality: Leahy (1981, 1983) has shown that there is a noticeable shift in these descriptions from a focus on peripheral characteristics, such as possessions or physical attributes, to a focus on social-psychological attributes, such as differences in personal effort or ability.

Explanations of preferred worker qualities were categorized based on the adolescents' general understanding of the relationship between the usefulness of a particular occupational skill or personal trait and successful job performance. It should be noted that the adolescents' description of either occupational skills or personal traits was not as important as the explanation of the relevancy of the particular skill or trait for job performance.

Thirty-one percent of these explanations were characterized as globally relevant, indicating a general awareness of the usefulness of a job-related skill or trait without an understanding of the specific relationship between the skill or trait and adequate job performance. For example, the following explanation was provided by a fifteen-year-old boy regarding the importance of being responsible: "[Workers] should be responsible, be responsible about their work." This explanation identifies responsibility as an important worker characteristic, but it does not *justify* its importance in terms of job performance.

In contrast, 27 percent of the adolescents were capable of providing one relevant explanation, while 42 percent of the adolescents provided multiple explanations. For example, a seventeen-year-old boy explains self-confidence in a worker in this way: "Self-confidence [is important]; if a person doesn't believe in themself or their abilities then their work is not good, they won't care about the job." In such explanations, students were able to make a coordination, lacking in more global responses, between personal traits or ability and social functioning relative to work performance.

Significant age differences were noted for these explanations of worker qualities. Specifically, twelve-year-olds provided greater proportions of global explanations (40 percent), compared to 32 percent of fifteen- and 20 percent of eighteen-year-old students. A corresponding increase in the number of multiple responses was demonstrated, with 57 percent of eighteen-year-olds, compared to 25 percent of twelve- and 44 percent of fifteen-year-old students, providing this form of response. Interestingly, the proportion of single explanations showed a modest decrease with age, perhaps reflecting the sizable changes in multiple explanations for this item.

Comprehension of the Concepts of Work, Career, and Occupation. In a review of career development literature, Super and Hall (1978) point out several problems surrounding inconsistent usage of the terms "work," "career," and "occupation." This inconsistency prompted Super and Hall to conclude that the apparent differences among vocational development models lies in the lack of agreement about these fundamental concepts.

In addition, Jahoda's (1982) summary of her research on adult employment indicates considerable diversity in adult perception of work concepts. According to Jahoda, work was described in three ways: (1) as a contractual agreement—that is, labor being provided for a fee; (2) as a goal-directed activity for the purpose of accomplishing a task; or (3) as an informal economic activity, such as housework. By contrast, careers were often described as encompassing the life span, as work histories consisting of different occupations, goals, and achievements leading to self-fulfillment. Occupations were commonly understood as general job categories that label a set of tasks common to a particular job.

Given the conceptual inconsistencies evident in the adult literature, we felt that an examination of adolescents' comprehension of these concepts from a developmental perspective would be appropriate. Thus, we analyzed adolescents' explanations of the terms "work," "career," and "occupation" using Jahoda's data on adults' perceptions of these terms. In explaining the term "work," 70 percent of the adolescents provided explanations reflecting one of the three explanations provided by adults. Most adolescents focused on the contractual nature of work—"a job task to fulfill [an] obligation to your boss for money," "something you do to earn a living" or on work as a goal-directed activity: "doing something [a task] in an effort to accomplish something."

A modest proportion of the adolescents surveyed (19 percent) demonstrated confusion about the concepts of work, career, and occupation. These students described work simply as a specific occupation at which a person works—"a doctor, lawyer, you know a job"—or as a career—"something you do [in life] to achieve your life goals, fulfillment." In addition, 11 percent of the adolescents either claimed they tried not to work whenever possible—"work is something to avoid"—or were unable to describe work adequately.

An analysis of possible developmental changes in these conceptions of work indicated a significant interaction between age and sex, with girls showing slightly more advanced explanations of work at age fifteen (in terms of mean score), than at age eighteen. Boys, however, showed a consistent gradual increase in comprehension (as expressed by mean scores) of the concept of work. The findings may reflect basic differences in sex-role socialization relative to occupational aspirations. Past research suggests that sex differences in occupational aspirations and attainment are related to traditional sex-role values regarding career orientation, marriage, and family expectations in adult life (Marini, 1978).

Adolescents' comprehension of career showed a similar general trend: 70 percent of the students surveyed provided adultlike descriptions of careers—"a job chosen to pursue for a prolonged period of time," "what you'll do for the rest of your life"—while 22 percent confused career with either work or occupation, and 8 percent were unable to explain clearly what a career is.

Significant age differences were noted in these explanations of career. Only 54 percent of the twelve-year-old students, compared to 74 percent of fifteen- and 84 percent of eighteen-year-old students, demonstrated an adultlike understanding of careers. Slightly over one-third (36 percent) of the twelve-year-old students described careers as either work or an occupation, while 10 percent were unable to describe adequately their perception of a career. In contrast, 17 percent of fifteen- and only 10 percent of eighteen-year-old students were unable to distinguish career from work or occupation, with even smaller proportions (9 percent of fifteen- and 6 percent of eighteen-year-olds) being unable to describe a career adequately.

Only 53 percent of adolescents were capable of providing adultlike conceptions of the term "occupation": 32 percent confused an occupation with either work or career, while 15 percent were unable to describe adequately what an occupation is.

These proportions also showed significant age effects. Although the proportions of adultlike conceptions of occupation showed an increase with age, the pattern of change was not as dramatic as changes in understanding of work and career. Specifically, only 45 percent of the twelve-year-old students, compared to 56 percent of fifteen- and 57 percent of eighteen-year-old students, demonstrated an adultlike understanding of occupation. The proportion of adolescents confusing occupation with work or career remained relatively stable (at one-third) across the three age groups. The proportion of adolescents unable to describe any aspect of occupation declined from a high of 25 percent at age twelve, to 11 percent for fifteen-year-old and 9 percent for eighteen-year-old students.

Discussion of Results. Age differences for these employment items support previous research (Goldstein and Oldham, 1979) outlining the transformation of work perception from fantasy-based notions of work typical of childhood to reality-based notions of adult employment. Our results also suggest that age-related changes in perceptions of worker qualities and in concepts of work, career, and occupation involve a growing awareness and understanding of the details of adult employment.

Although no significant age differences were found for descriptions of preferred worker qualities, explanations of these qualities were found to be highly related to age. Overall, younger adolescents gave a considerably larger proportion of global responses, indicating only a general awareness of worker qualities from the employer's perspective. With age, however, these naive perceptions of worker attributes were transformed into a coordinated understanding of the connection between personal roles, in the form of worker characteristics, and societal functioning relative to employment.

A more complex sex-age interaction was found for concepts of work. Significant differences between perceptions of work were demonstrated by fifteen-year-old boys and girls, with girls showing a relatively greater degree of understanding. This finding is somewhat perplexing given the clear age effects for responses related to concepts of career and occupation. A similar age effect was expected relative to comprehension of work, but the results did not support this expectation.

The result associated with the observed differences in work concept may be attributed to general sex differences in occupational socialization. Marini (1978) points out that the early occupational aspirations of preadolescents are unrealistically high for both boys and girls. These early aspirations undergo a number of changes during adolescence, and by early adulthood a more realistic assessment of occupational attainment is achieved. The data presented here may reflect the transformation in work concepts relative to traditional sex-role values. Boys are socialized to expect the pursuit of a career throughout their adult lives. Girls, however, receive conflicting messages. On the one hand, they are encouraged to pursue a career, but they are also cautioned about being too ambitious and risking failure in the traditional female roles associated with marriage and parenthood. Consequently, girls revise their aspirations downward in order to fulfill societal expectations.

These dymanics may account for the differences in comprehension of work concepts reported here. Girls may feel they need to choose between the two avenues—commitment to work or to family—during early adolescence. Boys, however, "know" their future—commitment to work—and do not feel the need to make occupational choices until later adolescence. This decision-making process may contribute to the divergence in the development of an understanding of work concepts, while career and occupation concepts are viewed in a more uniform manner.

Adolescents' Perceptions of Unemployment. Similar analyses were performed on the items measuring adolescents' perceptions of unemployment.

Causes of Unemployment. The adolescents in our study were asked to describe and explain both the general and personal causes of unemployment. Descriptions of each form of unemployment were categorized, using a modified version of Furnham's (1982a) adult descriptions of unemployment. In his study, adults described unemployment as due to individualistic causes—that is, personal inadequacies, such as poor education and training or lack of effort. Societal causes, with an emphasis on changes at the social-structural level—for example, poor industrial planning, competition from overseas, automation, or global ecomonic trends—were also perceived as contributing to unemployment.

Descriptions of the general causes of unemployment emphasizing the societal dimension were given by 66 percent of the adolescents. These descriptions typically focused on global economic problems—"prices are too high, inflation"; "people have no money [to buy goods], businesses have no money for materials or to pay workers"; overseas competition; "foreign imports are better than American products"—or on increasing technology ("robots and computers are taking over jobs").

In comparison, individualistic causes were mentioned by 19 percent of the adolescents, while 15 percent gave combined responses emphasizing both societal and individualistic causes. Descriptions of individualistic causes were exclusively of personal inadequacies: "They were lazy employees, didn't want to work," or "they didn't have enough education or appropriate training." Combined responses were descriptions of societal changes contributing to individual causes of unemployment; as one seventeen-year-old boy describes, "There is too much technology taking over jobs and people are unskilled for the technology."

Results associated with descriptions of the *personal* causes of unemployment showed a considerable proportion of adolescents' responses (90 percent) to be descriptions of individualistic causes. Descriptions relating to societal causes of unemployment were given by 7 percent of the adolescents, while 3 percent gave combined descriptions focusing on the relationship between both societal and individualistic causes.

Statistical analyses indicated no significant age differences for these descriptions of the general and personal causes of unemployment. These findings suggest that adolescents possess similar knowledge of the general societal and individualistic conditions leading to unemployment. Although adolescents' knowledge of the conditions of unemployment seems comparable across the age groups, one question still remains: Are there possible differences in understanding relative to their general knowledge of unemployment?

To examine this question, we analyzed adolescents' *explanations* of the causes of unemployment. It was found that these explanations ranged from a global awareness of the cause of unemployment without understanding the relationship between the stated cause and unemployment other than co-occurrence. For example, a fifteen-year-old boy explains that unemployment occurs "because there are no jobs." This may be true, but an explanation of such a general nature does not indicate an understanding of why unemployment occurs—that is, why there are "no jobs."

In contrast, explanations indicating an analytic understanding of the relationship between a particular societal or individualistic cause reflect a coordinated perception of the antecedents and consequences of unemployment. This coordinated understanding of unemployment is portrayed by a response from a seventeen-year-old girl: "[Unemployment] happens when advances in technology [no longer] make jobs available. [People] are insufficiently trained for jobs."

Significant age effects were noted for the adolescents' explanations of both the general and personal causes of unemployment. Findings associated with perceptions of general causes indicated a significant interaction between age and social class. Close examination of these findings indicated that adolescents from middle-class families demonstrated a greater (as indicated by mean scores) baseline level of understanding of the general causes of unemployment, while working-class adolescents showed considerable growth in understanding across the age groups.

Results associated with the adolescents' understanding of personal causes showed a more direct relationship between age and understanding. Nearly three-fourths (72 percent) of the twelve-year-olds, compared to 45 percent of the fifteen-year-olds and 35 percent of the eighteen-year-olds provided global explanations of the personal causes of unemployment. These proportions changed considerably with age, with 65 percent of the eighteen-year-old students demonstrating a more analytic understanding of the personal causes of unemployment, compared to 28 percent of the twelve-year-olds and 55 percent of the fifteen-year-olds.

Effects of Unemployment. Perhaps one of the most devastating consequences of unemployment is its effect on personal functioning. The adolescents were asked to comment on their perceptions and understanding of the general effects of unemployment on personal life. Descriptions typically centered on general changes in material conditions or personality traits resulting from unemployment. Descriptions of changes in material conditions focused on the effect of unemployment on the quality of life. Descriptions of personality changes focused on the personal-psychological consequences of unemployment. For example, an eighteen-year-old girl claims, "They [the unemployed] may have a bad attitude towards those with jobs. Could be jealous of people that are working."

Overall, 65 percent of the adolescents focused on changes in personality or behavior, while 27 percent described the relative influence of unemployment on the material aspects of personal life. In addition, 8 percent provided combined descriptions of the changes in both material and personal conditions.

No significant age differences were noted for these descriptions, but these data showed a trend similar to that of the descriptions of preferred worker qualities: Descriptions of the changes in material conditions of unemployed persons showed a decrease with age, while descriptions of the personal-psychological effects of unemployment increased.

This trend is also similar to findings reported by Furnham (1982b) and Leahy (1981, 1983) regarding descriptions of poverty and social inequality. In these studies, younger adolescents typically described differences between the rich and poor relative to personal possessions or material conditions. Older adolescents, however, focused on status differences due to social-psychological characteristics. The age trends reported here provide limited support of a general trend in the development of social understanding: Perceptions of personal and societal roles seem to move from an emphasis on external attributes toward a consideration of social-psychological differences among individuals within society.

Explanations of the effects of unemployment show a significant age trend similar to explanations of the causes of unemployment: a gradual transformation from global awareness of the changes associated with unemployment toward an analytic understanding of how unemployment causes change in either material conditions or personal behavior. Specifically, a sizable proportion (69 percent) of twelve-year-old students, compared to 56 percent of fifteen-year-olds and 50 percent of eighteen-year-olds, provided global explanations. Typically, these explanations did not adequately explain the relationship between unemployment and the particular effect other than co-occurrence: For example, a sixteen-year-old boy claims, "Unemployed people sleep all day, watch TV, and eat constantly." This response does indicate a general relationship between unemployment and personal behavior, but the adolescent is unable to draw any reasonable connection between unemployment and the stated behavioral change.

In contrast, a more analytic approach to these phenomena demonstrated a clear connection between unemployment and correlated changes in personality or possessions. The following example for a seventeen-year-old boy shows this difference in approach: "[Unemployed people feel] it's personally degrading to be working and then lose your job. They feel helpless, like they have no control over the situation." In this case, unemployment has been identified as contributing to a lack of self-worth and helplessness. This more analytic approach was demonstrated by only 31 percent of twelve-year-old students, compared to 44 percent of fifteen-year-olds and 50 percent of eighteen-year-old students.

Perceptions of Helping the Unemployed. Descriptions of the forms of aid available to the unemployed were either forms of personal aid or support given directly to an unemployed person by another individual—for example, "I would lend them money," or "I would be their friend, be kind to them." Forms of social aid were descriptions of relief emanating directly from social institutions—for example, "government should create new work programs," or "industry should help retain workers by retraining them."

Overall, descriptions of personal or societal aid were contributed in equal proportions; 45 percent of the adolescents emphasized personal aid, and 45 percent emphasized societal aid. Ten percent of the adolescents provided combined descriptions. No significant age effects were cited for these descriptions; nearly equal proportions of personal or societal aid responses were given in each age group.

Adolescents' explanations of these descriptions, however, showed significant age differences. Again, twelve-year-old students contributed a sizable proportion (77 percent) of global responses; a typical response was "get them a job" or "give them money." Such explanations do provide a measure of assistance, but there is no connection between the intent of the aid and the underlying conditions of unemployment, such as emotional and financial strain within the family or unemployability due to lack of skill.

These latter characteristics, demonstrating a more mature perception, were evident in the explanations provided by older adolescents. Nearly two-thirds (61 percent) of the eighteen-year-old adolescents, compared to 46 percent of fifteen-year-old and 23 percent of the twelve-year-old students, were capable of an analytic approach. The response of this eighteen-year-old boy exemplifies this approach: "[Society needs to] start to understand the problems of being employed and unemployed, needs to have better schools and create more jobs."

Society's View of Unemployment. General descriptions of society's prevailing views of unemployment were solicited. These responses were categorized as individualistic or societal.

Overall, 70 percent of the adolescents suggested that people in society attribute individualistic reasons as the cause of unemployment. Only 23 percent of the adolescents referred to societal causes as the root of unemployment, while a small proportion (7 percent) described society's perspective on unemployment as related to both individualistic and societal reasons.

These proportions were drastically different from their own views expressed earlier regarding general causes of unemployment. Descriptions of the general causes of unemployment were predominantly societal. This shift in perspective is supported by past research regarding attributions of unemployment by employed and unemployed adults (Furnham, 1982a). Unemployed adults typically attributed their status to societal causes, while employed adults attributed unemployment to individualistic causes.

The adolescents in our study may have interpreted the item regarding general causes in terms of: "What conditions may contribute to *my* unemployment?" Attribution theory clearly states that individuals are more likely to justify their own behavior in terms of situational (societal) influences, while dispositional (individualistic) traits are typically invoked when describing what motivates others (Ross, 1977).

Discussion of Results. The reported age effects for perceptions of unemployment parallel past research in the areas of adolescent perceptions of poverty and unemployment (Furnham, 1982a, 1982b, 1985; Leahy, 1981, 1983; Webley and Wrigley, 1983). These studies clearly show that younger adolescents focus almost exclusively on external, observable aspects of persons when making judgments of social status or employment conditions. By late adolescence, however, these perceptions change, reflecting an understanding of the connection between the various social and psychological influences on personal life.

Although no significant age effects were found for descriptions of unemployment in our study, we did note that these descriptions followed this developmental trend. Significant age differences were found for explanations of the personal causes and effects of unemployment and for explanations of aid to unemployed persons. Results from these three dimensions indicated that younger adolescents typically demonstrated a global understanding of unemployment, showing an accurate but incomplete perception of the complexities of social reality. The increase in more analytic forms of social understanding demonstrated by older adolescents reflects the construction of a more differentiated view of these unemployment issues.

The interaction between age and social class for explanations of the general causes of unemployment showed a similar age effect, with an increase in understanding with age. This trend, however, was influenced by the relatively high scores of fifteen-year-old middle-class students and eighteen-year-old students from both classes. This apparent discontinuity in causes attributed to unemployment is somewhat surprising. Given the substantial number of unemployed persons at the working-class level in this region at the time of data collection, one would assume that working-class adolescents would demonstrate a more differentiated understanding of unemployment. Instead, the reverse occurred—middle-class students showed a greater understanding of unemployment at ages twelve and fifteen, with students from both classes reaching similar performance levels by age eighteen.

This effect may be due to the personal nature of discussing issues related to unemployment. The experience of unemployment at the working-class level may be sufficiently disturbing to the younger students that a discussion of unemployment is avoided. The greater understanding of the oldest working-class students may reflect a capacity to separate personal feelings from their responses to this item.

Logical Reasoning and Work Perception. The predominance of age effects on work perception may be due to two complementary processes: expanding social experiences related to age and the emergence of formal reasoning capacities. Up to this point, this chapter has focused exclusively on the relationship between age and social understanding. Age effects alone, however, cannot account for all changes in social understanding. Other developmental processes correlated with age may influence work perception but may not be as directly observed.

In addition to the four qualitatively distinct levels of social understanding, beginning in early childhood and ending in preadolescence, that Furth (1980) described, he hypothesized the existence of a fifth level of societal understanding, which becomes manifest during adolescence itself. According to Furth (1980), "this further level would be *analytic-systemic*. It would be characterized by a formal, general approach to societal events rather than the personal, particular one observed at level 4 (concrete-systemic)" (p. 87). This fifth level of societal understanding was considered an extension of earlier perceptions of society due, in part, to the development of mature reasoning and greater participation in society. This speculation suggests a fruitful analysis of the relationship between logical reasoning and societal understanding in the form of work perception.

In our study, we performed separate analyses to examine the relationship between logical reasoning and work perception while controlling for age effects. Although preliminary analyses indicated significant age effects for all four employment items, logical reasoning was found to have little influence on the adolescents' explanations of these issues. Comparisons between levels of logical reasoning and form of explanation with each age group show gradual increases in the number of adolescents providing advanced responses independent of logical-reasoning level.

Comparable analyses for the explanations of unemployment items show that logical reasoning was closely related to more analytical explanations of the general and personal causes of unemployment and of help provided to unemployed persons. Of particular interest is the performance of the twelve-year-old and eighteen-year-old students at level 1 (low) and level 3 (high) logical reasoning. Only a few of the twelve-year-old students at level 1 (eighteen percent of responses across five unemployment items) provided more advanced explanations of unemployment. This same trend was apparent for the eighteen-year-old students with level 1 abilities (30 percent of responses across five unemployment items).

A different trend is observed when comparing the performance of level 3 reasoners within these two age groups. Except for explanations of the general causes of unemployment, twelve-year-old students at level 3 did not demonstrate explanations of unemployment concordant with their advanced reasoning capacities (20 percent of responses across four unemployment items). In contrast, eighteen-year-old students at level 3 showed a greater understanding of unemployment across all five items (64 percent of responses).

This apparent discrepancy regarding the role of cognitive operations in social understanding may be clarified by describing the difference between emerging and consolidated formal reasoning abilities. Piaget (1972) restated his position regarding the onset of formal operations, asserting that more mature forms of logical thought may not be truly functional until age fifteen or beyond. Moreover, formal thought processes may only be evident in the person's area of expertise. Recent studies examining this hypothesis have shown a developmental lag between the application of logical abilities in the physical and social domain—namely, that formal reasoning is demonstrated on problems in the physical domain prior to being demonstrated in the social domain (Kuhn, Langer, Kohlberg, and Haan, 1977). A similar developmental lag may be evident in our study, with younger adolescents demonstrating this emergence in reasoning in the physical domain (in this case, on the task that measured logical reasoning), while older adolescents possess consolidated formal reasoning and are capable of applying it in either the physical or the social domain.

Logical reasoning clearly influenced explanations given for the unemployment items, whereas no relationship between reasoning capacities and employment understanding was found. These performance differences may reflect an underlying bias in traditional vocational socialization practices. Socialization for employment begins early in life, with occupational attainment being the positive goal of this training. Education for the prospect of unemployment is virtually nonexistent and is certainly considered a negative aspect of vocational training. Within this context, it is reasonable to assume that adolescents' understanding of employment is more advanced due to the supervised educational and experiential opportunities available to them.

Past research has clearly indicated that, by sixth grade, children are well informed about the sex-segregated nature of occupations and occupational prestige and, by late adolescence, have experienced part-time employment (Hamilton and Crouter, 1980; Tremaine and Schau, 1979).

By contrast, unemployment is an unknown. Thus, within this domain, formal reasoning abilities are utilized to bridge the gap between the familiar (employment) and the unfamiliar (unemployment). Formal reasoning provides the adolescent with the framework to apply what is relevant from their understanding of employment to their understanding of unemployment.

Conclusion

The general purpose of this study was to examine the development of work perception for a relational-developmental perspective. From this viewpoint, adolescents' perception and understanding of work and related areas varied across age and, to a limited extent, level of formal reasoning capacities. These findings indicate preliminary support for continued analysis of work perception from a relational-developmental perspective.

References

Furnham, A. "Explanations for Unemployment in Britain." *European Journal of Social Psychology*, 1982a, *12*, 335–352.

Furnham, A. "The Perception of Poverty Among Adolescents." *Journal of Adolescence*. 1982b, *5*, 135–148.

Furnham, A. "Youth Unemployment: A Review of the Literature." *Journal of Adolescence*, 1985, *8*, 109–124.

Furth, H. G. "Young Children's Understanding of Society." In H. McGurk (ed.), *Issues in Childhood Social Development*. London: Methuen, 1978.

Furth, H. G. *The World of Grown-Ups: Children's Conceptions of Society*. New York: Elsevier, 1980.

Goldstein, B., and Oldham, J. *Children and Work: A Study of Socialization*. New Brunswick, N.J.: Transaction Books, 1979.

Hamilton, S. F., and Crouter, A. C. "Work and Growth: A Review of Research on the Impact of Work Experience on Adolescent Development." *Journal of Youth and Adolescence*, 1980, *9*, 323–338.

Jahoda, M. *Employment and Unemployment: A Social-Psychological Analysis*. New York: Cambridge University Press, 1982.

Kohlberg, L. "Moral Stages and Moralization: The Cognitive-Developmental Approach." In T. Lickona (ed.), *Moral Development and Behavior: Theory, Research, and Social Issues*. New York: Holt, Rinehart & Winston, 1976.

Kuhn, P., Langer, J., Kohlberg, L., and Haan, N. S. "The Development of Formal Operations in Logical and Moral Judgment." *Genetic Psychology Monographs*, 1977, *95*, 97–188.

Leahy, R. L. "The Development of the Conception of Economic Inequality: I. Descriptions and Comparisons of Rich and Poor People." *Child Development*, 1981, *52*, 523–532.

49

Leahy, R. L. "The Development of the Conception of Economic Inequality: II. Explanations, Justifications, and Concepts of Social Mobility and Change." *Developmental Psychology*, 1983, *19*, 111–125.

Marini, M. M. "Sex Differences in the Determination of Adolescent Aspirations: A Review of Research." *Sex Roles*, 1978, *4*, 723–753.

Meacham, J. A., and Santilli, N. R. (eds.). *Social Development in Youth: Structure and Content*. Basel, Switzerland: Karger, 1981.

Piaget, J. "Intellectual Evolution from Adolescence to Adulthood." *Human Development*, 1972, *15*, 1–12.

Ross, L. "The Intuitive Psychologist and His Shortcomings." In L. Berkowitz (ed.), *Advances in Experimental Social Psychology*. Vol. 10. New York: Academic Press, 1977.

Santilli, N. R. "Social Class and Paternal Employment Status in Adolescent Work Perception: A Developmental Approach." Unpublished doctoral dissertation, Catholic University of America, 1985.

Steinberg, L. D., Greenberger, E., Jacobi, M., and Garduque, L. "Early Work Experience: A Partial Antidote for Adolescent Egocentrism." *Journal of Youth and Adolescence*, 1981, *10*, 141–157.

Super, D. E., and Hall, D. T. "Career Development: Exploration and Planning." *Annual Review of Psychology*, 1978, *29*, 333–372.

Tremaine, L. S., and Schau, C. G. "Sex-Role Aspects in the Development of Children's Vocational Knowledge." *Journal of Vocational Behavior*, 1979, *14*, 317–328.

Vondracek, F. W., and Lerner, R. M. "Vocational Role Development in Adolescence." In B. B. Wolman (ed.), *Handbook of Developmental Psychology*. Englewood Cliffs, N.J.: Prentice-Hall, 1982.

Webley, P., and Wrigley, V. "The Development of Conceptions of Unemployment Among Adolescents." *Journal of Adolescence*, 1983, *6*, 317–328.

Youniss, J. E., and Smollar, J. *Adolescent Relations with Mothers, Fathers, and Friends*. Chicago: University of Chicago Press, 1985.

Nicholas R. Santilli is visiting assistant professor of psychology at Augustana College, Rock Island, Illinois.

Hans G. Furth is professor of psychology at the Center for the Study of Youth Development, Catholic University of America, Washington, D.C.

Young people's attitudes toward new technology are largely
pragmatic rather than evaluative and are strongly related
to psychological factors as well as to educational and
familial background.

Young People's Attitudes Toward New Technology: Source and Structure

Glynis M. Breakwell, Christopher Fife-Schaw

There are good reasons for us to study attitudes toward new technology if we are to understand the assimilation of young people into the world of work. The International Labor Organization of the United Nations (1985), in reporting on the integration of youth into working life, described how the basic structure of employment is changing under pressure from new technology. On the one hand, there is the worldwide decline of the industrial manufacturing base, compounded by the stagnation in the supply of public service jobs. On the other, there is the growth of the "quality of life" industries, such as recreation or secondary health care, especially those feeding off the microelectronic and biochemical revolutions. The report predicted that, as a result, unemployment internationally will rise and that there will be intensified polarization between those with and those without technological skills.

The expansion of the high-technology industries calls for a smaller but more scientifically and technologically qualified labor force, which,

The research reported in this chapter was supported by a grant from the Leverhulme Trust.

J. H. Lewko (ed.). *How Children and Adolescents View the World of Work.*
New Directions for Child Development, no. 35. San Francisco: Jossey-Bass, Spring 1987.

even if relatively unsophisticated, must be "machine-friendly." Already there is a definite shortage of skilled labor; for instance, in Great Britain, West Germany, Switzerland, and Japan, the limited number of computer programmers and software specialists is said to be slowing the diffusion of microelectronics. Young people entering the labor market for the first time are facing a widening disparity between what the education system provides and the demands made on them in jobs.

Acknowledgment of the educational and training deficits in relation to new technology has led many governments to initiate new schemes. The United Nations report called for greater flexibility in training programs, which should become more responsive to industrial needs through planning in collaboration with entrepreneurs. Implicit in this call for vocationally oriented education is the assumption that intermittent retraining will be necessary as market forces and technological advances modify the labor demand.

Such reorientation of both secondary and higher education to cater to the predicted needs of industry, which is now common in Western industrialized countries, has its critics. Many doubt whether industry can accurately predict sufficiently far in advance what training and skill requirements it will have in order for long-term educational planning to be dependent on it. Also, cynics suggest that industry may be deliberately overestimating its real requirements in order to flood the market with qualified labor and depress wage levels.

Despite this possibility, it is fairly clear that a larger technologically skilled work force is required; the doubts are about its precise size, not about the need for an increase. It is also clear that governments assume that people can be transplanted into such work as long as training and education are provided. This policy is founded on the further assumption that, if training is offered, it will be accepted. Such assumptions fail to consider the occupational aspirations of those meant to be trained. More important, they seriously underestimate the importance of attitudes held about new technologies. Governments seem to take for granted that clever young people who, in the past, studied social sciences or the arts can be switched to another line simply by closing courses in humanities and opening others in technology. They seem to believe that young people treat different types of careers as interchangeable. This belief is largely untenable. Young people choose work and training to accord with their system of sociopolitical beliefs and their values (Cotgrove, 1982). We might assume, then, that their existing attitudes to new technology would be predictive of their occupational aspirations and of their response to calls for the switch to science or engineering. Indeed, the former at least has been shown to be the case (Breakwell, Fife-Schaw, Lee, and Spencer, in press). Description of these attitudes therefore becomes relevant to both policy and practice.

The Definition of New Technology

Before describing young people's attitudes toward new technology, we think it sensible to attempt some definition of it. Yet new technology is an amorphous concept. There is little agreement as to what technology is but even less when its novelty needs to be judged. Sir Austin Pearce, head of British Aerospace, defines technology as "know-how," and this concretizes the *Concise Oxford English Dictionary* description of it as "the science of practical or industrial arts" or "the application of science."

Decisions about the newness of a technology are highly subjective and are dependent upon fear, familiarity, and usefulness, among other things, as much as on chronology. Nevertheless, there exists some consensus as to the major components of new technology, and this consensus emphasizes the microelectronic developments that have transformed information processing, communications systems, and automated routines. Recently, there has been an increasing awareness that bioengineering, particularly in relation to genetic engineering, is part of the new technology. Thus, we could say that we have what Moscovici (1985) calls a social representation of new technology: a system of beliefs and interpretative explanations of it that are generated socially through interaction and that impose meaning on the amorphous concept. The precise structure of the social representation of new technology does differ according to the economic and social position of the group from which it emanates; however, most adults have a sufficiently strong image of new technology that they are able to articulate their attitudes toward it as an entity.

Young people, in the age range from fourteen to eighteen, will also express views about new technology. As part of the work described in this chapter, 1,751 British schoolchildren in this age group were asked to indicate, from a checklist of sixteen products and processes, which ones they thought were new technologies. This list included some that were new in chronological terms (such as communication through fiber-optic cables, word processing, and genetic engineering), others that were not (such as brain surgery, bricklaying, and nuclear power generation), and some that were not clearly identified as one or the other (such as satellite communications links and freeze-drying).

The data were analyzed by frequencies and were multidimensionally scaled using the Smallest-Space Analysis (SSAI). The young people's decisions as to what constituted a new technology were not made entirely on the basis of actual age of technology. Attributions of novelty had more to do with familiarity than chronology; thus, microwave ovens were regarded as new less frequently than brain surgery. The table of perceived newness ran: laser surgery, fiber optics, computer-aided learning, satellite communications links, genetic engineering, nuclear power generation, brain surgery, robotic welding, word processing, microwave cooking, radar tracking, turbocharging engines, X-ray scanning, freeze-drying, plant breeding, and, finally, bricklaying.

The total number of processes selected as new varied according to sex and age. Boys thought significantly more things were new than girls, and there was an increase in the number perceived as new with increasing age. Also, those taking more scientific subjects for examination, regardless of sex, saw more new technologies in the list. If accuracy of decisions is examined, the sex difference disappears: Girls may choose less, but they are just as accurate because boys are overinclusive. Age increases accuracy, as does possession of computer literacy. (See Spencer, Fife-Schaw, Breakwell, and Lee, 1986, for a detailed description of findings.)

Gender, age, and scientific training, in the fourteen to eighteen age range, all appear to influence what is considered to comprise new technology. This finding is obviously important in interpreting attitudes expressed toward new technology. Any differences in attitude between the sexes or between groups with different scientific backgrounds or different levels of familiarity with computers is paralleled by differences in the very conception of new technology by the constituents.

The Structure of Adult Attitudes
Toward New Technology

Recent opinion polls (Mills, 1985) show that adult beliefs about new technology have a complex structure. They appear to reflect a differentiated cost-benefit analysis. While most adults believe that the microelectronic revolution will cause widespread unemployment, the loss of job skills, and consequent industrial unrest, they also believe that these changes should be accepted and claim that they would cooperate in effecting them. Although jobs are seen to be lost with the introduction of new technology, the actual reorganization of those that remain is viewed positively, the revision of working life is approached with equanimity, and it is expected to be essential for national economic prosperity. Attitudes toward new technology are, therefore, not unidimensional. They are founded on a network of beliefs, sometimes ill informed, that tends to produce ambivalence or, more likely, a multidimensional evaluation of new technology.

Breakwell, Fife-Schaw, Lee, and Spencer (1986) conducted an exploratory investigation of the structure of such attitudes in a sample of 534 undergraduates, with a mean age of twenty, using a series of Likert-scaled items about new technology. Factor analysis revealed five virtually independent dimensions that could be reliably scaled. These were: a general benefits factor, an inevitability of new technology factor, a protechnological training factor, a "green issues" factor, and a video games factor. General benefits indexed how far new technology was expected to bring improvements in domestic and working life. The inevitability factor measured how far innovations in technology can be considered inescapable.

The protraining factor indicated how far a career in industry and a technological education were considered desirable. The "green issues" factor related to expressed concern with those debates on armaments and pollution championed by the European "Green" political parties. The video games factor simply measured how much such pursuits were deemed valuable or disruptive. The relative independence of these factors supports the notion that attitudes toward new technology are multidimensional.

Data generated by university undergraduates have obvious problems of generalizability. Therefore, another smaller sample of adults with mixed occupational and educational backgrounds was contacted. The same five dimensions in attitudes to new technology reliably appeared; the multidimensionality is not some artifact of a highly educated sample.

Adult Attitudes Toward New Technology and Other Socioeconomic Beliefs

Cotgrove (1982) has argued that attitudes toward industry and science fit into broader sociopolitical belief systems. In fact, attitudes toward new technology do seem to be closely related to socioeconomic beliefs. Breakwell, Fife-Schaw, Lee, and Spencer (1986) examined the relationship between beliefs on the five dimensions and degree of conservatism and level of acceptance of the Protestant work ethic (Mirels and Garrett, 1971). The Protestant work ethic (PWE) is said to reflect the extent to which hard work is valued, and it correlates significantly with conservatism. Perhaps not surprisingly, greater conservatism and PWE are associated with a more positive attitude toward the general benefits of new technology, the inevitability of innovation, and the importance of gaining technological training. Conservatism was negatively correlated with concern for "green issues," as would be expected if the latter truly measures some preference for liberal or left-wing positions on environmental and peace issues. In short, attitudes toward new technology do seem to be enmeshed in broader socioeconomic beliefs.

Governments whose policy it is to encourage more young people to work in new technology need to examine seriously the implications of this finding (Breakwell, Fife-Schaw, and Lee, 1985). It suggests that modifying views of new technology and subsequent occupational aspirations may not be so simple because such modification may impinge on socioeconomic beliefs that are central to the individual's core concept of social identity and to his or her world view. Resistance to redistribution across training programs and employment may be mediated by negative attitudes toward new technology, but these, in turn, are anchored in political orientations that may well be antithetical to the governments' introducing change. Thus policy makers not only have before them the task of changing beliefs about new technology but also the need to unhook those beliefs from their political overtones.

Effects of Gender and Training on Attitudes
Toward New Technology

In the university sample, it was possible to explore the effects of gender and training on attitudes toward new technology since the sample contained roughly equal numbers of men and women and representative proportions from each of four areas of study: physical sciences, biological sciences, engineering, and human studies. The *only* gender differences that, though small, were significant were that men believed that there would be greater general benefits and that video games were valuable. Course of study related to willingness to train in technology: As would be expected, engineers were the most in favor of technological training, and the human studies students were the least; the latter were more concerned with "green issues" than the physical or engineering scientists. There were no other effects of course of study.

It is important to note that there were no sex-by-course-of-study interactions in dictating attitudes. Girls, overall, regardless of department, were less convinced of the general benefits of new technology than men, while engineers, regardless of sex, were more protraining. The female engineers, of whom there were very few, consequently had to maintain simultaneously that the benefits of technology are limited while adhering to the need to train for it.

There was one further finding of interest: There were no changes in attitude across the four years of university career. Admittedly, this assertion is based on cross sectional rather than longitudinal data and consequently must be treated cautiously. However, it is the case that engineers in the final year were not more in favor of technological training than those in the first year, and the human studies students were just as interested in "green issues" at the start of their university career as at its close. Apparently, students arrive at university with an attitude configuration that is maintained. The implication is that the university is not acting to socialize the student into a pattern of attitudes. Attitudes probably precipitate the student's choice of course of study.

Clearly, it would be rash to assert a causal relationship between attitudes toward new technology and choice of university course. Although they are correlated, both may be the product of some other cause without being themselves causally related. This applies also to the finding that attitudes toward new technology predict occupational aspirations (Breakwell, Fife-Schaw, Lee, and Spencer, in press). It could easily be that both are shaped by earlier events at school and in the home. Certainly it is the case that having taken examinations in science at school after fifteen years of age is associated with a more positive attitude toward new technology in adulthood (Fife-Schaw, Breakwell, Lee, and Spencer, in press [a]). This set of findings led to a series of detective exercises in schools to investigate the early sources of attitudes toward new technology.

The Structure of Schoolchildren's Attitudes
Toward New Technology

In this study, 842 boys and 903 girls of mixed ability, aged fourteen to eighteen years, from three British state coeducational schools, completed a questionnaire administered in large groups. The questionnaire gathered information on job aspirations, computer usage and literacy, educational background, and technology content of parental jobs, and it included scales measuring conservatism, the Protestant work ethic, self-esteem (Rosenberg, 1965), and psychological well-being (Goldberg, 1972) besides the five dimensions of attitudes to new technology. The questionnaire, though relatively long, took about forty minutes to complete, and even the youngest and least academically able had little difficulty in doing so.

Using this information, we took the first step in the process of detection, which was to establish the structure of attitudes toward new technology for this younger age group. First, we found that schoolchildren have less structured or differentiated systems of beliefs about new technology than do adults. We examined the internal reliabilities (Cronbach's alpha) for each of the five scaled dimensions established for adults. Only one, that concerning video games, remained reliable for schoolchildren. This means that items that, in the adult sample, were seen to hang together (that is, the items that measure a single attitudinal configuration) failed to do so for the children. The children did not respond to the group of items that referred to the general benefits of technology as if these items had a common focus and should be answered in a consistent manner, nor did they treat the inevitability, the "green issues," or the training dimensions as identifiable and separate constellations.

When the reliabilities of these scales were examined separately for children in each school year (fourth, fifth, and sixth formers—equivalent to ninth through twelfth graders in North America), it was further evident that there was no clear developmental trend toward the reliability of the scales. Older children saw no more meaningful connections among scale items than their younger colleagues.

Not surprisingly, therefore, factor analysis of the children's responses did not replicate the factor structure generated from the adults' data. More important, the factors discovered did not permit reliable scales to be constructed. However, SSAI indicated that the children did respond to a number of items from the original scales as if they formed aspects of a single belief system. This analysis revealed that some items that had originally formed part of the protechnology training and inevitability dimensions clustered together, while most of the others did not cluster together as expected or in an interpretable manner. Internal reliability analysis of those that did cluster established an eight-item scale that appears to measure the desirability of mastering technological advances and taking up appropriate training. It seems to reflect the desire to grab technological opportunities at the social and personal level: the motivation toward new technology. Examples of scale items include "everybody needs to be trained in computer use," "we should make every effort to use new technology to improve industrial efficiency," and "it is not important for everyone to understand the new technology."

It seems that schoolchildren do have a patterned system of beliefs about the use and mastery of new technology but not about its general benefits or its environmental and military implications. They focus on the pragmatic rather than on the evaluative level. They have a constellation of beliefs that fit together coherently and reliably where action in relation to new technology is concerned. Where values and broader assessments of social worth are concerned, their beliefs are unstructured and inconsistent.

This lack of structure in relation to beliefs about the sociopolitical implications of new technology is echoed in the absence of reliability in responses to the conservatism scale used. For the schoolchildren, the conservatism items did not appear to fall into a simple pattern. They were treated as separate items, rather than as symbolic of some underlying dimension of belief ranging from radical to reactionary. The children displayed no organized system of sociopolitical beliefs. It could, therefore, be argued that these fourteen- to eighteen-year-olds have not crystallized a system of consistent sociopolitical beliefs in relation to any target, and new technology is just one such target. New technology is seen as an arena of training and skill, as techniques with pragmatic value, and is considered of personal relevance; in this way, opinions about its mastery are systematized. In contrast, the sociopolitical context of new technology has not been developed. Of course, this may be good news for governments wishing to influence motivation without entering the domain of political debate.

Limitations in the Notion of Consistency

Before going on to examine the correlates of motivation toward new technology, we must take a short cautionary detour. Assertions about the structure of attitudes toward new technology have been founded on standard psychometric approaches: factor analysis, reliability analyses, and multidimensional scaling. On this basis, we can argue that young people have a unidimensional attitude toward new technology that concerns the importance or otherwise of mastery. Other dimensions, appearing regularly in adult populations, do not appear for fourteen- to eighteen-year-olds. However, the notion of consistency, or patterned responding, that underlies this conclusion has limitations.

In fact, it represents only one of three possible types of consistency in relation to attitudes frequently considered in social psychological literature. It concerns logical consistency in responses to a number of items (most frequently, these are simple statements with which the respondent expresses a degree of agreement or disagreement) at a single time. The second involves consistency in expression of opinion over a period of time. The third involves the consistency of expressed opinions with actions.

The survey data allow us to say that young people lack consistency of the first type in relation to sociopolitical beliefs, especially those associated with new technology. They do not allow anything to be said about the second and third types of consistency. Consequently, there is the possibility that the apparent absence of structure in attitudes to new technology is due to our failure to examine the young people over time or in action. The structure may appear in the fact that their beliefs, although unpatterned at a single time, remain constant over time or change in a systematic manner. The point is that the analysis reported offers information on only one sort of structural feature: constellations of belief at a single time. Recognizing this limitation, we are currently studying these young people longitudinally, but these data are as yet unavailable. When complete, the longitudinal study will permit statements about all three types of consistency.

In spite of the absence of longitudinal data, it should perhaps come as no real surprise that we failed to detect well-structured sociopolitical beliefs in our young subjects. There is quite strong current evidence to show that young people in this age group have little allegiance to traditional political groupings and great ignorance of political and social issues (Breakwell, 1986). Billig and Cochrane (1985), after an in-depth study of the political socialization of adolescents, argue that their views are inconsistent both over time and at any one time and are unrelated to action. The present data seem to confirm these findings.

The Sources of Motivation
Toward New Technology

For the time being, we will consider young people's attitudes toward new technology to revolve around the motivational factor, which amounts to a unidimensional view of new technology concerned with mastery. The next step along the detective trail is to examine the correlates of such motivation in order to ascertain its origins.

Basically, regardless of age, girls were significantly less likely to be motivated to control new technology. But there is also a significant effect for school year—the sixth formers (sixteen to eighteen years old) being most motivated, followed by the fourth formers (fourteen to fifteen years old), and with the fifth formers (fifteen to sixteen years old) being least interested in it. Presumably this effect is a product of self-selection for the sixth form by people interested in gaining further technical training, since education is not compulsory for British children after the age of sixteen.

Only the fifth and sixth formers completed the measures of self-esteem and psychological well-being. In order to examine the relative importance of these psychological factors in what follows, only data from the fifth and sixth forms will be presented ($n = 604$ girls, 518 boys). The self-esteem scale measured the overall sense of personal worth and confidence that the individual felt. The psychological well-being scale was derived from Goldberg's (1972) general health questionnaire, which was designed to measure risk of minor psychiatric morbidity. The psychological well-being scale is actually an index of the extent of anxiety or worry currently occupying the respondents. It encompasses some reference also to how well they feel they can cope with the anxieties they have. Self-esteem and psychological well-being are known to be correlated; however, they are by no means synonymous, and they proved to be significantly but not very strongly correlated ($r = 0.21$) in this sample. There is, therefore, reason to include both measures in the analysis.

The Protestant work ethic (Mirels and Garrett, 1971) scale, which indexes the intrinsic value attributed to employment and which had been found instructive in the adult sample, was also included in the analysis. Since the motivation measure is concerned with gaining mastery and training, we expected that it would be highly related to PWE, which indicates interest in industriousness, application, and hard work.

It was found that motivation correlated significantly with self-esteem, psychological well-being, and PWE ($r = -0.18$, -0.07, and 0.21, respectively, $n = 1,122$). Greater motivation was associated with more self-esteem, better well-being, and stronger PWE. The correlation pattern possibly reflected the perceived self-potential for mastery and the motivation for seeking it. The PWE places a value upon work and success that might provide the motive for the protechnology orientation; at the same time, higher levels of self-esteem and psychological well-being might encourage one to believe that personally gaining control of new technology is within one's powers and thus worth considering.

In searching for the origins of the protechnology attitude, we made one discovery that seems particularly important. This relates to familial background rather than to psychological factors. The young people were asked to describe to what extent their parents' jobs involved new technology. There were five levels of technological involvement, ranging from none at all to a lot, with a sixth category to cater to the parents without paid employment. It was found that, regardless of sex, those with "high-tech" fathers were more likely to be motivated to master technology. The range includes: very high tech, medium high tech, unemployed, low tech, no tech—with those who did not know the technological content of their father's job least interested in mastering new technology.

The technology content of mothers' jobs had no significant relationship to motivation. The technology content of fathers' and mothers' jobs were related in an unsurprising manner, which supports the argument that the perceptions of the children are accurate. Overall, few women were perceived to have more new technology in their work than their husbands did. Also, those children who considered their fathers to have high-tech jobs were proportionally more likely to have mothers who were not in paid employment. The fact that their responses parallel the actual pattern of male and female employment in new technology is useful validation of the children's perceptions. Obviously, it is still possible that the perception of parental work could be influenced by the individual's degree of motivation. In other words, it might be that high motivation shapes the perception of the father's job so that it is portrayed as possessing more new technology. However, it would be difficult then to explain why the mother's job should not also be subjected to this reconceptualization, especially by highly motivated girls. Moreover, it would be difficult to explain the medium levels of motivation for the offspring of unemployed fathers. Although the direction of causality for this finding cannot be definitely established, it seems likely that it is the new technology content of the father's job that influences motivation rather than motivation that produces the perception of the father's job. This interpretation is further supported by the finding that those whose fathers were deemed to have high-tech jobs were more likely to possess home computers. High-tech fathers provide both a role model and facilities at home for their children to practice relevant skills.

These analyses, while describing the data accurately, do not show the relative importance of the psychological and familial variables. In order to do so, a $2 \times 3 \times 6$ analysis of covariance, using sex, school year, and technology content of father's job as independent factors, and self-esteem, psychological well-being, and PWE as covariants, was carried out on motivation scores. The resulting analysis showed that self-esteem, PWE, school year, sex, and perceptions of the technological content of father's job all contribute independently to motivation scores. As suggested by the pattern of correlations mentioned above, PWE and self-esteem both share small proportions of variation with motivation toward new technology, but, independent of this, motivation scores are associated with year of study and perceptions of father's job.

The value of this more integrated analysis is to show the relative importance of factors in predicting levels of motivation. The PWE comes first, self-esteem second, year of school third, father's job fourth, with sex trailing behind and accounting for only a small, barely significant portion of the variability in motivation. Psychological well-being scores fail to contribute to the prediction of motivation in any serious way.

The way that sex of respondent becomes of minimal importance in explaining variability in motivation must be explained. There is a significant sex difference in motivation, as well as in self-esteem: Young women have markedly lower levels of self-esteem, and the analysis shows that the difference between the sexes in motivation is largely attributable to the variations between them in self-esteem. It is self-esteem, rather than gender, that is the best predictor of motivation. Taken with PWE, self-esteem accounts for a large amount of the variation in scores on motivation. It is the fact that self-esteem is correlated with psychological well-being which means that the latter fails to improve the prediction of motivation once the former has been extracted.

It is interesting that this analysis of covariance points to the primacy of two psychological factors in determining motivation. Such a finding may have practical relevance for any government keen to accentuate motivation relating to new technology. The psychological factors are, after all, substantially easier to influence than the structural features like gender, age, or home background. Anyone interested in equal employment opportunities for women might also take heart from the finding, although it does give rise to the problem of how to improve women's self-esteem.

It might be worthwhile reiterating why PWE and self-esteem might be expected to produce high motivation. PWE provides the motive for desiring mastery of new technology by emphasizing the importance of work, particularly the kind of work that is highly valued by mass society. With the current emphasis on technology, PWE naturally would be channeled into the motivation toward technological work. Self-esteem provides the psychological basis for believing oneself capable of acquiring skills deemed difficult to gain and considered valuable. Hence, self-esteem should and does engender motivation. This is the rationalization for the assumed direction of causality, with PWE and self-esteem as sources of motivation.

Implications of Motivation for Action

So far, this discussion has revolved around the possible sources of motivation toward new technology. The next step in the analysis is to examine the implications that such motivation has for behavior. Understanding the action import of such motivation is fundamentally important. As a reflection of a state of mind, the new technology motivation may be interesting, but, if it can be shown to be a predictor of behavior, it becomes much more valuable.

In fact, there is a clear relationship between protechnology motivation and school subject choice. Fourth and fifth formers (fourteen- to sixteen-year-olds) taking science O-levels (the nationally standardized public examinations taken in Britain at sixteen years of age) are significantly more motivated than those taking none. In the sixth form (sixteen- to eighteen-year-olds), those with more science O-levels are more motivated, and those taking science A-levels (public examinations taken in Britain at eighteen years of age) are most motivated. This pattern applies equally to both girls and boys taking science subjects.

It is also evident that motivation scores are related to the amount of computer usage and computer literacy (as indexed by the number of computer languages known). The young people were asked about the frequency of computer usage at school, home computer ownership and usage, types of use made of computers, number of programming languages known, and where they had learned to use the machine. The results of these questions are presented in Fife-Schaw, Breakwell, Lee, and Spencer (in press [b]). They showed that 80 percent of pupils used school computers less than monthly or not at all. Confirming previous findings, the study showed that girls are much less likely than boys to use the school's computing facilities (Siann and Macleod, 1985; Hoyles, 1985; Turkle, 1984). Also, only about 40 percent of the girls, compared with over 60 percent of the boys, had a computer where they lived. Presumably this would reinforce the school trend toward lower usage by girls. Only 1 percent of girls reported being able to use more than one computer language, compared with 16 percent of boys, while the figures for one language are 22 percent for girls and 42 percent for boys. In terms of type of usage, the data suggest that, while playing games is by far the most popular use for computers, it may also serve an interest-maintenance function that facilitates progression to more complete use of the computer's powers and to the learning of programming languages. Higher levels of motivation are associated with more frequent usage, greater computer literacy, and more diverse and advanced types of usage of the machines. These effects apply independently of gender.

Occupational aspirations are also related to motivation toward new technology. Respondents indicated what jobs they would like to have after leaving school. These were categorized according to the likely technological content. A seven-category taxonomy resulted that was found to be manageable, if not perfect. The categories were: talent/artistic/creative; welfare/people oriented; office/commercial services; service industries; high tech/scientific; security/armed services; academic; and a no-clear-idea group. There were manifest gender differences in aspirations. Young women were much more likely to aspire to welfare or people-oriented jobs (nurse, teacher, social worker, probation officer, and so on) than young men. The girls were much less likely to aspire the high-tech/scientific jobs (computing, scientific research, telecommunications, aerospace industry, and so on). Instead, they opted for office services (secretary, clerk, receptionist, telephone operator, and so on). Trends across age groups were weak and few. High-tech jobs became relatively more attractive as the pupils got older, while service jobs lost popularity. This finding, however, is obviously related to the fact that the older pupils have the higher educational attainment that is required for training in science and technology. The effects of motivational orientation cut across age and gender. Higher motivation scores are associated with a desire to enter the high-tech/scientific jobs. Highly motivated young people shun welfare or people-oriented work.

The motivation to master new technology, therefore, appears to be tied to scientific orientation at school, level of computer usage and literacy, and occupational aspirations. Again, there is the question of causality, but, in this context, it seems rather pointless. It is likely that at least scientific orientation and computer usage are dialectically related to motivation, and occupational aspirations are probably also related in this way. That is to say, scientific orientation, computer usage, and occupational aspirations are evolved over a long period of time; they grow and change in accordance with context and at the insistence of experience. There is no reason to believe that the protechnology motivation is any less reflexive. In fact, all four might be expected to interact with each other to bring about mutual reconstruction. This process of continual interaction and reformulation is at the heart of the statement that they are dialectically related.

Another possibility needs to be considered: that motivation, together with scientific orientation, occupational aspirations, and computer usage, is merely a function of intellect. The argument would then be that intelligent young people are motivated to control new technology, to choose technological jobs and science examinations, and to have more to do with computers. No direct measure of intelligence was taken in our survey, but examination successes can be taken to reflect intelligence, at least of one sort. It is true that students studying sciences at the O-level tend to have more O-level passes than those not studying more than one science. This is partly a product of the way pupils are allowed to make subject choices by the school authority. However, it is not true that pupils wanting technological jobs or using computers more or with greater fluency are likely to have more examination successes. Most important, motivation is not directly related to sheer number of overall examination successes, though it is related to the number of successes in science subjects. Level of academic ability, though doubtless an ingredient, cannot act as the single explanation of the linkages among the four variables.

The closeness of the motivation index to the other variables, especially scientific orientation, gives pause for thought. If the particular value of measuring motivation lies in its power to predict behavior, it is only worthwhile doing so if it can then make predictions not viable on the basis of other indices. It is possible to test the independent predictive power of the motivation index holding scientific orientation constant because, among those with a number of science successes in the sixth form, there is variability in motivation scores. Not *all* those with a scientific orientation in school subjects show high levels of motivation. It might be hypothesized that, if motivation has an independent contribution to make to the prediction of behavior, where scientific orientation is held constant, variability in it will be related to occupational aspirations and computer literacy. In fact, it was the case, that, among sixth formers taking only science A-levels, motivation scores were predictive of aspirations for technological employment.

Motivation and the Perception of New Technology

Our detective work has so far established that motivation is related to PWE and self-esteem, affected by the technology content of father's job, and varies with age and gender. We have also discovered that motivation is associated with a scientific orientation at school, relatively frequent computer usage and programming abilities, and occupational aspirations involving technology. Now we can return to the issue of the definition of new technology.

We have already explained that respondents specified which of a checklist of sixteen processes or products they regarded as new technology. Some of these were, on a chronological criterion, actually new, some old, some indeterminate. In order to examine the relation of motivation to perceptions of new technology, we compared the responses on the checklist of those in the upper and those in the lower quartiles on the motivation scale, using the frequency analyses and SSAI. We found that the highly motivated children perceived significantly more of the processes in the checklist to be new technologies, and they were more accurate in identifying those that were new in chronological terms.

In examining the two-dimensional SSAI plots of the pattern of responses, we found (from the coefficients of alienation and the scatter) that members of the highly motivated group have a more highly organized, coherent perception of what constitutes new technology: Not-new and relatively ordinary methods are tightly clustered, and the new technologies are scattered along the second dimension, which reflects distinctions made about the high- or low-status connotation of the process. In contrast, the low-motivation group shows a much less systematic perception: The old technologies do not cluster closely, and some processes are clearly and consensually misperceived as old—for instance, word processing and genetic engineering. It is notable that members of the low-motivation group are significantly more likely to fail to see word processing, genetic engineering, fiber-optics communication, and computer-aided learning as new technologies. Given the rate at which these technologies are transforming the economic and social context of young people, we find such inaccuracy illuminating. The unwillingness to try to master new technology is associated with uncertainty as to what it constitutes. This implies that the motivation factor is tied to a particular perception or social representation of new technology. Low-motivation young people actually conceive of new technology differently, at the concrete rather than at the evaluative level. This may, of course, explain why they do not wish to

66

master it. Highly motivated young people believe that they are setting out to master a different set of things from those that the low-motivation students reject.

Some Conclusions About Attitudes
Toward New Technology

Our detective hunt has led to a number of conclusions about attitudes toward new technology in young people: Their attitude is unidimensional but pragmatic and instrumental rather than being founded on any sociopolitical evaluation. It concerns the need for mastery of new technology, not the drive to assess its socioeconomic benefits or disadvantages. Some young people want mastery, others do not, and this is tied to their conception of what new technology is. Those dismissing the need for mastery are inaccurate in their perceptions of new technology. Moreover, they have low PWE and low self-esteem, which, indeed, may explain why they would not be motivated toward mastery or feel capable of achieving it. The desire for mastery grows with age and is greater in males, and it is related to the nature of the father's job. Fathers with high-tech jobs provide their children with a role model and tend to provide computer facilities at home, which, in turn, engender skill development and help motivate children toward mastery of new technology. Scores on motivation toward new technology are predictive of scientific orientation at school, computer usage and literacy, and occupational aspirations.

If we are to understand young people's approach to work and integration into the labor market, then the way they relate to new technology will become increasingly important over the next few years as government policies to retrain and redistribute labor are implemented. The work reported here represents a preliminary analysis of the connections among the perception of new technology, attitudes toward it, underlying psychological factors, work values, familial background, educational experiences, and job aspirations. Without doubt, the analysis shows that, with regard to new technology, as with other targets, social cognitions—which comprise the interpretations and evaluations of all information—are directly connected to the individual's biography and plans for action.

References

Billig, M., and Cochrane, R. "Political Socialization." Paper presented at the Economic and Social Research Council Social Beliefs Conference, Cambridge, England, March 1985.

Breakwell, G. M. "Political and Attributional Responses of the Young Short-Term Unemployed." *Political Psychology*, 1986, 7 (3).

Breakwell, G. M., Fife-Schaw, C., and Lee, T. R. "Young People's Attitudes to New Technology: Their Policy Implications." *Science and Public Policy*, 1985, *12* (6), 337–340.

Breakwell, G. M., Fife-Schaw, C., Lee, T. R., and Spencer, J. "Attitudes to New Technology in Relation to Social Beliefs and Group Memberships." *Current Psychological Research and Reviews,* 1986, 5 (1), 34–47.

Breakwell, G. M., Fife-Schaw, C., Lee, T. R., and Spencer, J. "Occupational Aspirations and Attitudes to New Technology." *Journal of Occupational Psychology,* in press.

Cotgrove, S. *Catastrophe or Cornucopia?* New York: Wiley, 1982.

Fife-Schaw, C., Breakwell, G. M., Lee, T. R., and Spencer, J. "Attitudes Toward New Technology in Relation to Scientific Orientation at School: A Preliminary Study of Undergraduates." *British Journal of Educational Psychology,* in press (a).

Fife-Schaw, C., Breakwell, G. M., Lee, T. R., and Spencer, J. "Patterns of Teenage Computer Usage." *Journal of Computer-Assisted Learning,* in press (b).

Goldberg, D. *The Detection of Psychiatric Illness by Questionnaire.* Oxford, England: Oxford University Press, 1972.

Hoyles, C. "The Learning Machine: The Gender Gap." BBC Television broadcast, September 5, 1985.

International Labor Organization of the United Nations. *Integration of Youth into Working Life.* United Nations Working Paper. New York: International Labor Organization of the United Nations, 1985.

Mills, S. C. "British Attitudes to New Technology." *Economic and Social Research Council Newsletter,* 1985, *55,* 24–26.

Mirels, H. L., and Garrett, J. B. "Protestant Ethic as a Personality Variable." *Journal of Consulting Clinical Psychology,* 1971, *36* (1), 40–44.

Moscovici, S. "On the Phenomena of Social Representations." In R. Farr and S. Moscovici (eds.), *Social Representations.* Cambridge, England: Cambridge University Press, 1985.

Rosenberg, M. *Society and Adolescent Self-Image.* Princeton, N.J.: Princeton University Press, 1965.

Siann, G., and Macleod, H. "Are Computers Girl-Friendly? The Origin of Gender Differences in the Response to Computer Technology." Paper presented at the British Psychological Society Social Section Conference, Clare College, Cambridge, England, September 1985.

Spencer, J., Fife-Schaw, C., Breakwell, G. M., and Lee, T. R. "Representations of New Technology." Working Paper No. 2. Surrey, England: Department of Psychology, University of Surrey, 1986.

Turkle, S. *The Second Self: Computers and the Human Spirit.* New York: Granada, 1984.

Glynis M. Breakwell is director of the Leverhulme project on young people's attitudes toward new technology and is a lecturer in social psychology at the University of Surrey, Guildford, Surrey, England.

Christopher Fife-Schaw is a research fellow in the Department of Psychology, University of Surrey, Guildford, Surrey, England.

*Longitudinal studies of parents experiencing unemployment
and economic instability indicate how unstable the family
context may be for the children, affecting their health and
behavior and, very likely, their ideas about the world of work.*

The Family Economic
Environment as a Context for
Children's Development

Dale Clark Farran, Lewis H. Margolis

A recent review by Rutter (1983) of stress and its effects on children suggests that the only events so far established to be associated with negative reactions in children are ones that affect the child directly. Examples of these kinds of events are hospitalization of a week or more under the age of five, the birth of a sibling, and parental divorce. To that list of directly, seriously disruptive events, a review by Farran and Cooper (1986) added foster-care placement and institutionalization.

These events share the following features: First, they directly disrupt the social interactions of the children, in some cases substituting an entirely new social system for the one to which the children are accustomed. Second, they involve either a permanent or at least lengthy change in children's habitual routines, and, third, they may change the children's view of themselves and their ability to cope. But even these extensive changes have not been firmly linked to particular behavioral outcomes for all children who experience them.

Farran and Cooper (1986) have summarized evidence to show that severely disruptive events do affect children's later social interactions—at a minimum, disrupting peer relations and, at the most extreme, creating

J. H. Lewko (ed.). *How Children and Adolescents View the World of Work.*
New Directions for Child Development, no. 35. San Francisco: Jossey-Bass, Spring 1987.

problems with severe aggression. But these authors also recognized that not all children showed the same effects from similar events. Some children appear to be more vulnerable to disruptive experiences; these tend to be males, children who have negative temperaments, and those whose family backgrounds include alcoholism, schizophrenia, or criminality. Thus, to determine the effect of any particular event on children, researchers must take into account extensive information about the children and their backgrounds (see for example, Werner and Smith, 1982).

Another difficulty in determining the connection between an event and any subsequent behavioral difficulty is that *both* may be the result of other events or factors (Robins, 1983). This idea is an extension of the vulnerability thesis: Disruptive events may happen to people because they are more vulnerable. Robins cites the work on divorce as an example; most research has found a relationship between divorce and behavioral difficulties in the children. Yet Robins cites evidence to show that psychiatrically disturbed adults are more likely to divorce. Children of psychiatrically disturbed adults are more likely to have adjustment problems, whether or not their parents divorce. In such a situation, it is extremely difficult to determine what separate influence the divorce is exerting.

Children indeed represent a special problem in determining the effects of other events. Since children live nested in families, frequently the positive or negative aspects of an event are determined for the child by how the adults are reacting, as Burlingham and Freud (1942) illustrated in their study of children who survived the blitz bombing in London. Feinman and Lewis (1984) have termed this dependence on others for one's reactions as "social referencing"; they believe that it can first be seen in infants who are six to twelve months of age. In other words, in order to know how an event is being experienced by children, we may need to understand first how their parents are reacting to and then how they are communicating the event. Both observable parental reactions and their direct communications to children are part of social referencing.

Thus, it appears that the only events uniformly associated with later behavioral outcomes for children are those that directly affect the child. Yet, even with these events, other factors modify a conclusion of predictable connections between the child's perceptions and behavior and the events being experienced.

Parental Unemployment: An Indirect Stressor

In contrast to events that directly impact the child are *family* events that, through their disruption of the family, may, in turn, affect the child adversely. Patterson (1983) has argued that the family system, not children, is directly at risk because of such stress. But, when the family system is upset or disrupted, then children may have adjustment problems; the family system determines the ultimate adjustment of the child. If Patterson is correct, events that appear to be more indirect for the child may actually have strong effects if they strongly influence the parents.

One possible event of this type is parental unemployment, an event of some magnitude for the person losing the job. In 1981, Margolis and Farran (1984) surveyed families where the father had recently lost his job due to an unexpected closing of part of a plant. Parents reported illness rates in their children two to ten times higher than parents from an area of the plant that did not close.

Pautler (1984) surveyed children's worries in a sample of sixth, ninth, and twelfth graders in a community beginning to recover from a period of unemployment. Concerns about extended paternal unemployment, repeated paternal unemployment, and insufficient family money were confined to those children whose fathers had experienced job loss during the past twelve months. The other children, however, did express concerns about job prospects after high school and/or college and about not having enough personal money, leading the investigators to suggest that economic uncertainty, regardless of paternal work status, has an impact on children.

There is further evidence to show that even the anticipation of a negative family event can cause disruption. An early analysis of the data presented in this chapter demonstrated a relationship between job security and child health (Margolis and Farran, 1984). At the first interview, fifty-five employed fathers were asked to rate their job security. The children whose fathers reported low job security had illness rates six times higher than those of the children whose fathers felt secure in their jobs.

Numbers of Children Who Experience Various Stressors

The loss of a job by one of their parents happens to many more children than other more directly stressful events. An examination of the numbers of children who experience various stressors in a given year revealed that about one-tenth of 1 percent of children in this country will go through the trauma of losing a parent through death; another 1.7 percent will experience their parents divorcing (Glick, 1979). In a given year 5.3 percent will suffer a serious illness (Select Panel for the Promotion of Child Health, 1981). Based on the above data, three times as many children (more than 15 percent) will experience parental job loss, and ten times as many will go through a divorce as will experience hospitalization.

Thus, parental unemployment is an important area to study. First, this research can elucidate a heretofore relatively neglected family crisis involving quite a large number of children. Second, it may help researchers understand the "ripple" effect of an adult event on other family members.

The rest of this chapter focuses on children in varying economic circumstances. In about half the families, the father had recently become unemployed through plant closings or layoffs. The other families were from similar plants and were living in the same community as unemployment rose. Our interest in this longitudinal project was in determining the effects of various economic crises, job loss being the most extreme, on the children in the families involved. Studying this area in general and, specifically, studying these factors longitudinally proved more troublesome than might at first be imagined, and the study has helped us to identify a number of variables that should be considered in future research on children and the work world.

Defining the Family Economic Environment

Job Status of Parents. Previous investigations of the influence of the economic environment on adults have generally focused on two dimensions. The first dimension is employment status, which is usually defined as either working or not working at the time of a particular interview or encounter. A further refinement of the definition of working differentiates those working for, say, more than thirty hours per week from those working fewer hours.

A variation on work status is the duration of unemployment at the time of an interview. Cobb and Kasl (1977), have suggested that the duration of joblessness affects individuals in a manner that may differ from the experience of losing a job. Stated alternatively, the risk to an individual's health and well-being probably differ when there are, for example, three job losses of one month's duration in contrast to one job loss of three months' duration, even though both experiences constitute three months of joblessness.

The second major dimension of the economic environment is income level, or more precisely, per-capita income for the household. Countless studies have documented the detrimental effects on health and development of having a low income (for example, Starfield, 1982; Gortmaker, 1979). A variation on the income dimension is to measure the change in income. Elder (1974), for example, uses a decline in income of 30 percent to signify "economic deprivation" in studies based on the Oakland child development data.

Work status and income are obviously related. In 1980, the median income for all husband-wife families was $24,020 (Terry, 1982). For those families that experienced unemployment by the wife only, the median income was $21,455, a difference of 11 percent. For those families that experienced unemployment by the husband only, the median income was $17,432, a difference of nearly 28 percent.

Since fathers traditionally have been the sole or major breadwinner for families, analyses have generally been restricted to work status and percapita income based on the father's situation. (Snyder and Nowak, 1984, recently provided evidence that the effects of unemployment may be different for male compared to female job losers). The steady rise in the proportion of women who work outside the home makes it necessary to include the mother's work status and income when attempting to characterize the family's or children's economic circumstances. A mother working outside the home has at least two potential types of influences on her children: One influence is psychological/sociological; factors such as the mother's variety of roles from wage earner to homemaker, her time both away from and at home, and her relationship with her husband and with others have been described as influences on children's development (Bronfenbrenner and Crouter, 1983). A second influence is economic; mother's employment brings economic benefits that may also influence the children (Ferber and Birnbaum, 1982).

Thus, the major dimensions of the child's economic environment include work status of both the father and the mother as well as the duration of unemployment for those without jobs who are seeking them. Furthermore, the incomes of both parents constitute the family income. Although job loss by a father generally results in a greater proportional decline in family income for two-earner families, the loss of a mother's income may also result in financial hardship for the family.

Other Related Factors. Although work status and income are traditionally the two factors most often utilized to characterize the family's economic environment, both empirical and theoretical studies suggest the need to describe economic circumstances in greater detail.

Fringe benefits represent a substantial contribution to income. On the average, for every dollar earned in wages, a worker earns an additional twenty-five to thirty cents in benefits such as health insurance and pension contributions (Best, 1981). Consequently, the loss of work-related fringe benefits constitutes a major loss of income. Additionally, because they are based on group rates, these benefits are either unavailable or prohibitively expensive when dissociated from the workplace.

Health insurance, potentially the most important benefit contributing to the children's well-being, is work related for approximately 80 percent of workers (Staines and Quinn, 1979). This benefit may end at the time of job loss or continue for a few months. Therefore, two workers who lose their jobs on the same day but from different companies may find themselves and their families in contrasting benefit situations. In addition, where two parents are working and are covered by insurance, the insurance of the continuously working parent may protect the family from a lapse in coverage. It is worth noting that, when health insurance coverage does lapse, public programs such as Medicaid do not adequately protect families.

Job security is another characteristic of the economic environment that may influence health and behavior. In their study of 100 terminees and 74 continuously working men, Cobb and Kasl (1977) noted that the time between announcement of a plant closing and the actual closing was stressful. During the preclosing time, workers anticipating job loss were found to have greater elevations in uric acid, cholesterol, and epinephrine, as well as increases in hypertension and joint swelling, compared to the stably employed.

A third factor that merits attention in study design and analysis is satisfaction with income. Depending on expectations and budgetary habits, workers and families may view the same income level as satisfactory or as wholly inadequate.

Measuring the Family Economic Environment

The magnitude of the problem of defining work or economic circumstances in a meaningful and statistically powerful way is demonstrated by a simple calculation of the cells possible when the six characteristics of the family work environment previously identified are defined as follows: Father's work status would include full-time, part-time, and unemployed. Mother's work status would include full-time, homemaker, and unemployed (in the market for a job but currently unemployed). Although income is a continuous variable, for the purposes of discussion, three levels are proposed with one level being below the poverty line. Families either have or do not have health insurance. Job security could be categorized as secure or not secure; similarly, for those who are laid off, their evaluation of the prospects of finding a job are either good or poor. Finally, families would be classified as either satisfied or dissatisfied with their household income. (For simplicity, only the father's benefits, job security, and job prospects are included.) The product of the cells indicates 216 possible combinations of factors or, in other words, 216 possible ways to categorize the economic environment of families, using even a relatively simple scheme.

The definition of the economic environment is further complicated by the fact that some of these factors have lagged effects. For example, Elder (1974) and Rutter (1983) have demonstrated that particular events, such as parental job loss, divorce, and parental death, may not manifest consequences for children for months or even years.

To illustrate the variability and changeability of the economic environment for children, we shall use the data from the North Carolina Work and Family Life (WFL) Project. Although numerous studies have examined the importance of the individual economic factors, we are not aware of other data sets that have investigated so many economic circumstances both simultaneously and over time.

Introduction to the Work and Family Life Project

The Community of Albreton. Albreton is an old, industrial city in the northeastern United States. The two-county metropolitan area from which the study sample was drawn has a population of 375,000. There are sizable Irish, Italian, and Eastern European ethnic groups; 97 percent of the residents are white. Many of the families have resided in the community and worked in the same plants for more than one generation, as evidenced by the fact that 67 percent of the target children had three or four grandparents born in the Albreton area, and only 6.7 percent had no grandparents born in the area.

The economy consists of a diverse industrial and agricultural base that has sustained a growth in the labor force from 153,000 to 181,600 over the past decade. In 1980, the year before the recent recession descended, 95 percent of the labor force was engaged in nonagricultural employment in the following categories: manufacture of durable goods (26 percent); manufacture of nondurable goods (15 percent); and nonmanufacturing (54 percent).

The diversity of Albreton's economy has, until recently, protected its families from widespread economic dislocations. Until 1981, the local unemployment rate remained consistently lower than the national figure. Even in 1975, the worst year of the previous recession, when the unemployment rate in Albreton rose to 7.8 percent, the rate was still below the national figure of 8.5 percent.

As the recession deepened in Albreton, the unemployment rate climbed from 7.3 percent in September 1981 to 9.9 percent in April 1982, the starting date of this project. By January 1983, the unemployment rate reached 16.1 percent. The rate subsequently declined slowly to 8.6 percent in September 1983, when the project came to a close.

Description of the Study Sample. The process of recruiting participants occurred in three stages. First, one of the project coordinators met with the labor advisory committee of the community. This group of eleven, chosen by the labor council to represent a cross section of the various crafts in the county, advised both the labor council and other community agencies on matters of community interest. The advisory committee strongly endorsed our project. The coordinator then met with many presidents of local unions who also supported this work.

The second stage involved obtaining layoff lists and work rosters from which to select participants. The third stage of enrollment involved telephoning individual families whose names appeared on the various rosters. The names on these lists generally appeared in order of seniority. Telephone recruitment was conducted by volunteer counselors from the labor advisory committee, persons very unfamiliar with survey research. When the family was contacted, an interviewer explained that he or she was calling from the labor advisory committee, which was trying to learn more about how families were dealing with the recent economic changes in the country. The interviewer then asked if there were children older than nineteen months and younger than thirteen years and if there were two parents in the home. If the interviewee answered in the affirmative, he or she was asked to participate in a series of interviews over the course of a year.

Approximately 26 percent of the individuals on the layoff lists and work rosters could not be contacted by telephone. Approximately 42 percent of those contacted were ineligible, mainly because they had no children or children of inappropriate age. Of the contacted eligibles, approximately 29 percent agreed to participate.

Given the limitations inherent in a small sample selected from a single geographic area, the WFL sample, nevertheless, corresponds well demographically to the general population of working individuals. In order to control for the effects of social class and family composition, we restricted the sample to blue-collar workers with two parents in the home and at least one child in the appropriate age range. Fathers ranged in age from twenty to forty-seven years with a mean of thirty-one years, and mothers ranged in age from twenty-two to forty-six years with a mean of thirty years. The mean number of grades completed was approximately twelve for both fathers and mothers. Although 21 percent of the fathers had completed at least one year of college, 50 percent had completed at least one vocational or technical course. For mothers, 16 percent had at least one year of college, and 35 percent had completed vocational or technical training. The mean number of household members was four, indicating two children with two parents.

Economic Characteristics of the Families

Initial Status. This analysis is based on 113 families for which there was complete information at three interviews on the six variables we have outlined: (1) father's work status; (2) mother's work status; (3) per-capita income; (4) health insurance; (5) father's job security; (6) satisfaction with family income.

At the first interview, 48 percent of the fathers were unemployed, and 52 percent were employed full-time. For all 113 families, 58 percent of the mothers were in the labor force (83 percent of those were employed, and 17 percent were unemployed but looking for work), and the other 42 percent were homemakers. The distribution of mother's work status was similar for employed and unemployed fathers. At the time of the first interview, then, this population reflected the demographics of the national labor force, except, of course, for the large proportion of unemployed fathers. (In order to control for the effects of duration of unemployment, only fathers with fewer than six months of unemployment were included in the sample.) The proportion of mothers in the labor force reflected the national figure.

For the purposes of this analysis, income has been divided into three categories. Families with per-capita income below the 1982 poverty standard ($9,682 per year or $47 per person per week) were assigned to the low-income group (L). Families with weekly per-capita income between the poverty level and 185 percent of that level ($87 per person per week) were assigned to a middle group (M). The figure 185 percent was utilized because that is the income level below which families would be eligible for the Special Supplemental Food Program for Women, Infants, and Children. Families with incomes above 185 percent of the poverty level were assigned to the high group (H).

Adding the income characteristics to the work status of the fathers and mothers begins to introduce considerable variation. Of the 113 families, 23 percent fell below the poverty line at the first interview. Ten percent of the families with employed fathers fell below the poverty line, and, as expected, a higher percentage (37 percent) of those with unemployed fathers fell below that level of income. Families with an unemployed father and homemaker mother had the highest proportion of families below the poverty line.

Interestingly, three families with both unemployed fathers and mothers managed to have household incomes that placed them in the upper-income group. In all three cases, either the mother or the father was laid off from a company that provided supplemental unemployment benefits that could raise benefits to 95 percent of prelayoff pay.

Of the 113 families in the study, 87 percent had health insurance. Those families with a single labor-force attachment—that is, a father in the labor force and a mother as a homemaker—were at significantly greater risk of being without health insurance when the father became unemployed.

Employed fathers were asked to rate their job security on a five-point scale. In this analysis, fathers who stated that their jobs were "pretty secure" or "very secure" were classified as secure in their jobs. Fathers who described their situations as "could be better, could be worse" or "not secure" or "a lot of talk about a layoff or closing" were classified as insecure in their jobs. This characteristic introduces a major division in the sample. Of the fifty-one full-time employed fathers who commented on job security, twenty-two (or 43 percent) felt insecure in their jobs.

Finally, parents were asked to state whether they were satisfied with their family income. Overall, 64 percent of the families expressed dissatisfaction with their current income. Among the fifty-two families with employed fathers, 40 percent expressed dissatisfaction. For the fifty-four families with jobless fathers, all but three were dissatisfied with their incomes.

The economic environments for the children at the time of the first interview were complex. The group of unemployed men were demographically similar to their employed peers. The similarity persisted when the mother's work status was introduced. If father's and mother's work status were the only significant economic circumstances, then assessment of the indirect effects of the family's economic environment on children's perceptions and behavior would appropriately take place by comparing the children of these unemployed fathers with those of the employed fathers. When the additional circumstances, such as income and job security, are introduced, however, the determination of comparable groups becomes problematic.

Changes by Second Interview. Not only is the economic environment quite variable but it is also unstable. Table 1 displays the change in work status of fathers and mothers over the course of our study. Between the first and second interviews (median duration of six months), 10 percent ($n = 6$) of the employed fathers experienced job loss, while 39 percent ($n = 21$) of the unemployed fathers returned to full-time work or part-time work. Twenty-five percent of the mothers experienced changes in work status between the two interviews. In the fifty-four families where the fathers were initially unemployed, 22 percent of the mothers subsequently made changes in their work status: Five of the twenty-five homemakers became employed, and five of the six unemployed mothers returned to work. Among the fifty-nine families where the father was employed at the beginning of the study, 30 percent of the mothers experienced changes in work status. Of the thirty-one employed mothers, six became homemakers and two became unemployed. Of the twenty-three homemakers, seven became employed, a figure comparable to the proportion of wives of unemployed husbands who gained jobs.

In summary, over 40 percent of the sample experienced changes in work status by either the father or the mother over the course of a few months. For the most part, these changes could be considered desirable, but six fathers and two mothers became newly unemployed.

Approximately 37 percent of the families experienced a change in income status between times 1 and 2. More than half of the changes were positive, from either low to middle or middle to high income. Of the eighteen families who experienced a drop in income, nine fell below the poverty level. The fact of father's employment does not necessarily protect children from declines in income. Nine of the families whose fathers were employed at time 1 experienced declines in income, but in only two cases was that due to loss of work by the father at time 2.

At time 2, twenty-three families were without health insurance, an increase from the eleven families at time 1. Three families lost health insurance when the fathers became unemployed. Seven families lost their health insurance when the fathers continued as unemployed and benefits

Table 1. Change in Parental Work Status over Time

A. Change in Fathers' Employment Status

Paternal Work Status at Time 1	Work Status at Time 2	
	Employed	Unemployed
Employed n = 59	53	6
Unemployed n = 54	21	33

B. Change in Mothers' Work Status Within Sample of Unemployed Fathers

Maternal Work Status at Time 1	Mothers' Work Status at Time 2		
	Employed	Unemployed	Homemaker
Employed n = 23	21	1	1
Unemployed n = 6	5	1	0
Homemaker n = 25	5	0	20

ran out. Nine families continued with no health insurance. Ironically, four families who had coverage while unemployed at time 1 were without coverage at time 2, even though the fathers became re-employed. In none of these cases was the coverage due to mother's employment. Presumably, health insurance was provided for a short period after a layoff or job loss and then subsequently lapsed. These newly re-employed fathers then either faced a waiting period before becoming eligible for health insurance or took jobs that did not provide that benefit.

Job security changed considerably from time 1 to time 2. The general level of insecurity remained virtually unchanged at 45 percent, but 25 percent of the fathers experienced a change. Of the fathers employed at both interviews, 15 percent became less secure in their jobs, but nearly as many (10 percent) became more secure in their jobs. Thirty-one percent remained insecure, and 44 percent remained secure in their jobs.

For the entire group, the proportion dissatisfied with their income did not change. Over 20 percent became dissatisfied with their incomes, while nearly 18 percent became satisfied. Slightly more than half of the families remained dissatisfied at both interviews. Of those twenty families that became satisfied with their incomes, only ten actually experienced an increase in income, with eight experiencing no change and two, interestingly enough, experiencing a decline in income, yet an increase in satisfaction.

Summary. It is clear that studying the effects of parental unemployment or studying the family's economic environment more generally will be an extremely complex undertaking. The fathers' unemployed status is obviously not the sole criterion by which families should be judged as having experienced important economic changes. Before we get to the point of measuring how the parents are reacting to the event of unemployment and thus interpreting it for the child, we need to obtain a clearer definition of the economic context in which the event is occurring. We also need to know to whom the family should be compared—other families who are employed but living below the poverty line; other families whose fathers are also unemployed but whose mothers are working and whose income is high; or some other category?

Our data show that the economic environment for children is not easy to characterize, nor is it stable. Both mothers and fathers are moving in and out of the work force; income and crucial benefits, such as health insurance, change over a six-month period. Perhaps this frequent shifting in economic status contributes to what has been reported as heightened anxiety in American children about their families compared to children in other countries (Bryant, 1986).

The following case studies illustrate the complexity of the problem. These are cases from our 113 families, chosen because they are representative of families experiencing paternal unemployment and because they illustrate the variety of reactions in families and children.

Four Families: Case Studies of
Changing Economic Environments

Each of the following cases has been chosen to represent a group of families undergoing somewhat similar experiences. There were other more extreme cases in our sample: One father, laid off at the beginning of our study, was unable to find work and began drinking heavily. He died of heart attack in February 1983. Another family's home was in the process of being sold at a sheriff's sale when we ended the project. Five families divorced during the course of the study (four whose fathers were unemployed, one in the employed group). This rate of severe disruption (death, home loss, divorce) is probably high, given a sample of 113 followed for only twelve to fifteen months. These cases are not going to be described in detail because they were not typical of what was happening to the group as a whole.

Each of the following case descriptions will provide selected data reflecting the economic environment of the family as well as a narrative description of what happened to the family over the course of the twelve to fifteen months of study, during which families were interviewed three times. In addition to descriptions of their economic situations, data were collected on the health and mood of the adults and the one target child in the family. Complete data on the family economic environment variables for the four cases over the three time periods are presented in Table 2.

Case A. The first family has three boys. The target child for our study was the youngest boy, who was twelve and was characterized as a "slow learner." The parents had been married for sixteen years. They had married young; when the study began, the father was thirty-three and the mother, twenty-nine. He had finished the ninth grade; she, the seventh.

Both parents were laid off when they entered the study in June 1982, but they did have health insurance. Their only source of income was unemployment compensation; they considered themselves to be under severe economic strain. To relieve the strain, the father took a part-time job and the mother took two part-time jobs.

The mother's work schedule resulted in role changes within the family as the father began providing more child care and more help with jobs around the house. Thus, an indirect stressor began to have direct consequences for the child in terms of how his family was organized. While this rearrangement of responsibilities might have been tolerated well in some families, it was not in this one. All three members of the family about whom we were getting information showed the strain at the second interview, with the father being the most affected.

According to the interviewer, this father was a "nervous wreck" during this period, losing twenty pounds from an already thin frame in three months. Having his wife bear such financial responsibility was unacceptable to him. His health was poor, and his mood was extremely negative. He was depressed, not sleeping, very resentful, and felt unsure of himself as a husband and father.

By the third interview, the situation was more normal for this family. The father was again working full-time; the mother had given up one of her part-time jobs. There were more role changes, as the mother regained control over child care and running the household. Both parents' mood scores were back to an average level, and the father reported few health problems.

During the study period, the target child, as would be expected, experienced a few more health problems than usual and slightly increased negative scores for behavior at home. Other than those reactions, however, he had a very good year. He did well in school, participated in the special olympics and won ribbons, and was on a winning baseball team.

What buffered this child from a severe stress in the family, reflected in changed roles for both parents and extreme upset by one? Being younger might have helped. More important perhaps was the fact that this was (according to the interviewer) a close, "family-oriented" set of parents, caring obviously for each other and for all three boys. Also important may have been the fact that the child was achieving success in several

Table 2. Family Economic Environments (FEE) for Four Case Studies

FEE Variables	Time Periods		
	1	2	3
Fathers' Work Status:			
Case A	Laid off	Work part-time (PT)	Work full-time (FT)
Case B	Laid off	Laid off	Laid off
Case C	Work FT	Laid off	Laid off
Case D	Laid off	Work FT	Laid off
Mothers' Work Status:			
Case A	Laid off	Work PT (2 jobs)	Work PT
Case B	Homemaker	Homemaker	Homemaker
Case C	Work PT	Homemaker	Homemaker
Case D	Work FT	Homemaker	Homemaker
Weekly Income:			
Case A	$198.00	$361.00	$370.00
Case B	$180.00	$180.00	$183.00
Case C	$240.00	$198.00	$198.00
Case D	$220.00	$215.00	$173.00
Health Insurance:			
Case A	Yes	Yes	Yes
Case B	No	No	No
Case C	Yes	No	No
Case D	Yes	Yes	Yes
Income Satisfaction:			
Case A	Dissatisfied	Dissatisfied	Satisfied
Case B	Dissatisfied	Dissatisfied	Dissatisfied
Case C	Dissatisfied	Dissatisfied	Dissatisfied
Case D	Dissatisfied	Dissatisfied	Dissatisfied
Fathers' Job Security (If Employed):			
Case A	Not applicable (NA)	NA	Very secure
Case B	NA	NA	NA
Case C	Very insecure	NA	NA
Case D	NA	Very secure	NA
Fathers' Work Opportunities (If Unemployed):			
Case A	Few jobs available	Jobs are available	NA
Case B	Few jobs available	No jobs available	No jobs available
Case C	NA	No jobs available	No jobs available
Case D	Jobs are available	NA	No jobs available

arenas outside the home. Rather than the home stress intruding on school and peer relationships, successes in those areas may have strengthened the boy's ability to cope at home.

Case B. This is a case of a responsible, concerned child who wanted to help out with the family finances. The target child was a twelve-year-old twin son of somewhat older parents; his mother was thirty-six, father forty-two when the study began. They had been married sixteen years. Neither had graduated from high school.

The father was laid off when we began the study and was without work the entire time. At one point, his unemployment benefits ran out, and the family applied for public assistance. He received an extension of his unemployment benefits, and they withdrew the application. As the study concluded, he was into his last week of eligibility for unemployment and was preparing to reapply for welfare. The mother did not work. (See Table 2 for complete economic environment data.)

The stress level over the year was very high for both parents. The father's physical health was normal for this group, but his mood scores reflected his upset. The mother's health was not good, and she scored as having one of the most negative moods of any mother in the sample. The boy, on the other hand, had good behavior at home. His grades at school were good and he received a merit certificate for Junior Fitness. He was reported to be doing odd jobs to save money to treat the family to outings. During the preceding year, he had earned enough from mowing lawns to send the family to Hershey Park. According to the interviewer, the parents, despite their health and mood problems, were very focused on the children. The interviewer reported that the two boys were the "center of concern and attention in this family."

The father's age and the seniority he held at his previous job operated against his finding a new job. His seniority also kept him hoping for a recall from the old plant. According to the interviewer, worrying about finances and the future kept the mother from eating and sleeping well. However, thus far the target child had coped well. How he and the family would handle public assistance was a major question when the study ended.

Case C. The third family was somewhat younger than the previous ones. The target child was a six-year-old girl whose father was working full-time when we first interviewed the family. He was laid off just before the second interview. (See Table 2 for complete data.) At the same time, the mother discovered she was pregnant and also stopped working. This family lost their health benefits immediately, and could not afford private coverage (and likely would not have been eligible, given the pregnancy). They gave birth to the new baby with no health coverage and incurred a $3,000 debt—a debt still owed at the close of the study.

These were young parents; the father was twenty-five, mother twenty-three. They had been married seven years but had not been able to afford to buy a home. Neither had graduated from high school.

Both parents were depressed and in very negative moods. Both had health problems, especially at the beginning of the study. The child also had health problems. She broke her arm at the same time as the layoff and the discovery of the pregnancy. Her illnesses were less dramatic for the rest of the year, though they continued to be above average in number. Her behavior scores were average.

This case presents a picture of a family struggling with economic adversity in the midst of the other kinds of events that also happen to young families. Youth, in other ways, may be on their side: At the end of the study year, the interviewer commented that the father still felt optimistic about his chances of finding work.

Case D. Unfortunately, the final family does not have the same note of optimism about it. These parents were also young (mother, twenty-six; father, twenty-eight). They had only been married for two years. Living with them was the mother's seven-year-old son from a previous marriage; this was the target child for our study. Shortly after our study began, the mother stopped work to give birth to a baby boy.

The father was laid off in the beginning of our study. By the second interview, he had found a replacement job and considered it quite secure. This security proved unfounded. He was laid off again by the third interview. The mother, who had stopped working to have the baby, was seriously thinking of returning to work at the close of the study. (See Table 2 for complete data on the family economic environment.)

One major contributor to the family's stress was the lack of a permanent living situation. They moved twice during the interview year, once from a small house on the property of the mother's parents to a wing inside the parents' home. The arguments with her parents were severe, however, forcing them to move to a small apartment. The maternal grandmother kept the seven-year-old at the beginning of the last move because she did not like the size of the new apartment, nor did she believe that her daughter was doing a good job of raising the child. The boy remained with his grandmother for only a short time before returning to the family.

The mother appeared to feel the stress the most. She listed many health problems for herself and responded highly negatively in the mood questionnaire. The interviewer felt that the mother was becoming seriously depressed and might be in need of medication.

Both children in the family had serious problems. Although we were not specifically following the newborn, we noted that he was hospitalized three times during his first year of life, once for high fevers, once for appendicitis, and a final time for bowel obstruction. The seven-year-old did not have such serious health problems—he had an unexplained cough that lingered for three months—but his behavior deteriorated, and there was a great deal of tension between him and his parents, especially after he spent time away from them at his grandmother's. The arguments between the parents about the child and about the work and living situations also increased dramatically.

For this family, the recession coincided with other major changes in their lives: a new marriage with barely time to get started, the problems for the father of creating a relationship with the stepchild, a sick infant, several major moves, and serious quarrels with their family. It is hard to imagine what internal or external factors these parents could have had that would have enabled them to cope with all of these demands.

Conclusion

A growing body of developmental research suggests that family stressors may increase the risk of a variety of detrimental outcomes for children. This research is based on a model that assumes that stressors such as divorce, hospitalization, and others are concise and clearly definable. We initiated our investigation into the health and behavioral consequences for children of parental unemployment assuming that we could characterize the exposure to job loss in a straightforward way. A job loss usually has a definite date, in contrast to a divorce, the proceedings for which may drag on for months or years. Similarly, work status, on the surface at least, appears to consist of basically two major categories—employed and unemployed. This contrasts with hospitalization, which is likely to be associated with a preceding illness of some duration and perhaps a period of disruptive convalescence.

Generally, the experiences of the families in the North Carolina Work and Family Life Project, as illustrated in the four case studies, suggest that work status and economic circumstances from the perspective of a child are both complex to define and constantly changing. As we have indicated, even a simple classification system of economic circumstances results in a myriad of permutations of conditions that may influence children's perceptions and behavior. Factoring in the mother's work status further complicates the characterization of the family's condition. Finally, these economic conditions are remarkably unstable, even over such a relatively short period of time as six to fifteen months.

The case studies that we have presented give a picture of the great variety of economic circumstances faced by working-class families during a time of economic recession. The father tended to be most affected by the economic changes that these families were experiencing; the mothers, in no cases the major breadwinners, were affected to a lesser degree than were the fathers. In contrast, the children in our samples seemed to cope reasonably well with the economic strain their families were experiencing. Evidence is accumulating from our study and others to suggest that the person to whom a potentially stressful event is occurring directly is most affected: men in the case of job loss (Cobb and Kasl, 1977); women in the case of separation and divorce (Kiecolt-Glaser and others, in press). There are no satisfactory models to capture the interaction of parental events, individual events, and developmental stages for children. It is difficult to support the notion of any "main effect" on children involved even in fairly dramatic family shifts.

Ongoing analysis is concerned with three questions and issues. First, given that job loss is an indirect stressor for children, we are exploring what consequences the various changes in economic circumstances had on family functioning that directly influenced the children. For example, we are examining the influence of job loss on family routines and the distribution of family roles. Second, although the parents in our study have all been affected by the job-loss experience, the distribution of responses leads to an exploration of the individual, family, and community support that modified the effects for many families. Finally, if paternal job loss does not have a meaningful direct effect on the children, it is important to examine which components and events in family, economic, and social environments do have an impact on their health and behavior.

In closing, we would like to underscore the importance of including family economic environment variables in studies that are examining the indirect effects on children of conditions in the adult work world. Embedded in the unstable family economic environment is information that children will use in formulating their own views of reality. By acknowledging the potential influence of such variables as loss of benefits on the child's emerging views of work and the family, we stand a much better chance of beginning to unravel this complex set of experiences.

References

Best, F. *Work Sharing.* Kalamazoo, Mich.: Institute for Employment Research, 1981.

Bronfenbrenner, U., and Crouter, A. C. "The Evolution of Environmental Models in Developmental Research." In P. H. Mussen (ed.), *Handbook of Childhood Psychology: History, Theories, and Methods. Vol. 1.* New York: Wiley, 1983.

Bryant, B. K. *The Neighborhood Walk: Sources of Support in Middle Childhood.* Chicago: University of Chicago Press, 1986.

Burlingham, D., and Freud, A. *Young Children in Wartime.* London: Allen & Unwin, 1942.

Cobb, S., and Kasl, S. *Termination: The Consequences of Job Loss.* Washington, D.C.: U.S. Department of Health, Education, and Welfare, 1977.

Elder, G. H. *Children of the Great Depression.* Chicago: University of Chicago Press, 1974.

Farran, D. C., and Cooper, D. "Psychosocial Risk: Which Early Experiences Are Important for Whom?" In D. C. Farran and J. D. McKinney (eds.), *Risk in Intellectual and Psychosocial Development.* New York: Academic Press, 1986.

Feinman, S., and Lewis, M. "Is There Social Life Beyond the Dyad?" In M. Lewis (ed.), *Beyond the Dyad*. New York: Plenum, 1984.

Ferber, M., and Birnbaum, B. "The Impact of Mother's Work on the Family as an Economic System." In S. Kamerman and C. Hayes (eds.), *Families That Work: Children in a Changing World*. Washington, D.C.: National Academy Press, 1982.

Glick, P. C. "Children of Divorced Parents in Demographic Perspective." *Journal of Social Issues*, 1979, *35*, 170.

Gortmaker, S. L. "Poverty and Infant Mortality in the United States." *American Social Review*, 1979, *44*, 280–297.

Kiecolt-Glaser, J., Fisher, L., Ogrocki, P., Stout, J., Speicher, C., and Glaser, R. "Marital Quality, Marital Disruption, and Immune Function." *Psychosomatic Medicine*, in press.

Margolis, L. H., and Farran, D. C. "Unemployment and Children." *International Journal of Mental Health*, 1984, *13*, 107–124.

Patterson, G. R. "Stress: A Change Agent for Family Process." In N. Garmezy and M. Rutter (eds.), *Stress, Coping, and Development in Children*. New York: McGraw-Hill, 1983.

Pautler, K. "Children's Worries and Perceptions of Work and the Future in Times of Economic Uncertainty." Unpublished master's thesis, Laurentian University, Sudbury, Ontario, Canada, 1984.

Robins, L. "Some Methodological Problems and Research Directions in the Study of the Effects of Stress on Children." In N. Garmezy and M. Rutter (eds.), *Stress, Coping, and Development in Children*. New York: McGraw-Hill, 1983.

Rutter, M. "Stress, Coping, and Development: Some Issues and Some Questions." In N. Garmezy and M. Rutter (eds.), *Stress, Coping, and Development in Children*. New York: McGraw-Hill, 1983.

Select Panel for the Promotion of Child Health. *Better Health for Our Children: A National Strategy*. 4 vols. Washington, D.C.: U.S. Government Printing Office, 1981.

Snyder, K., and Nowak, T. "Job Loss and Demoralization: Do Women Fare Better Than Men?" *International Journal of Mental Health*, 1984, *13*, 92–106.

Staines, G. L., and Quinn, R. P. "American Workers Evaluate the Quality of Their Jobs." *Monthly Labor Review*, 1979, *102*, 3–12.

Starfield, B. "Family Income, Ill Health, and Medical Care of U.S. Children." *Journal of Public Health Policy*, 1982, *3*, 244–259.

Terry, S. L. "Unemployment and Its Effect on Family Income in 1980." *Monthly Labor Review*, 1982, *105*, 35–43.

Werner, E. E., and Smith, R. S. *Vulnerable But Invincible: A Longitudinal Study of Resilient Children and Youth*. New York: McGraw-Hill, 1982.

Dale Clark Farran is head of the child development research department, Center for Development of Early Education, Kamehameha School, Honolulu, and associate professor of psychology, University of Hawaii.

Lewis H. Margolis is assistant professor, Department of Public Health and Policy Administration, University of Michigan.

The chapters in this sourcebook suggest important areas for further research.

Concluding Comments

John H. Lewko

Over the past three decades, we have seen a major structural change in the world economy, with foreign competition emerging on all fronts (Reich, 1983) along with growing concern about decreasing worker productivity. Structural unemployment is now considered a worldwide phenomenon (Garraty, 1978), and concepts such as "flexible-system production" and "dead-end labor" are emerging (Reich, 1983). Amid this turmoil, we have young people faced with the decision of what course of action to follow in the inevitable transition to adulthood. Their subjective experiences provides one critical source of information on which to base such a decision.

The information contained in this sourcebook demonstrates that children and adolescents are indeed monitoring the adult world, developing perspectives, and then acting on them. Piotrkowski and Stark have established the family as an important learning context regarding occupations and family-work conflict, while Breakwell and Fife-Schaw have demonstrated the potential influence of family in the formation of attitudes toward new technology. In both studies, the father's work experience played a major role. Farran and Margolis also illustrated the indirect link between the adult work environment and negative effects on the child. *How* the family functions to shape individual perceptions of the work world remains to be discovered. However, the broad range of family-child linkages presented in this volume, as well as emerging trends (such as

J. H. Lewko (ed.). *How Children and Adolescents View the World of Work.*
New Directions for Child Development, no. 35. San Francisco: Jossey-Bass, Spring 1987.

part-time employment) that add new dimensions to family circumstances, reinforces the need for further investigation.

While the family is clearly a major influence on children's subjective interpretations of the work world, the chapter by Santilli and Furth, along with the work of Youniss and Smollar (1985), leads us beyond the family to consider the broader network of social relationships available to the child and adolescent. A relational-developmental approach, such as that proposed by Santilli and Furth, draws our attention to the interpersonal relationship as the basis for interpreting the work world and to the need to include peers, employers, and teachers as potential forces in shaping perceptions of the work world. Indeed, the marked differences between the communitywide effects versus the individual family members effects on views of work in the Pautler and Lewko chapter could have arisen in part from the manner in which the peer group responded to the circumstances.

The relationship between perceptions of and actions involving the work world also merits close attention. The work of Breakwell and Fife-Schaw, for example, demonstrates a relationship between an orientation toward a mastery of new technology and a science orientation in school, computer usage and literacy, and occupational aspirations. On the other hand, the pattern of work attitudes identified in the Pautler and Lewko chapter, if acted on by adolescents, would lead to extremely counterproductive interactions with the work world. Such research is difficult and time consuming, but, without rigorous exploration of the link between beliefs and actions, our studies on children's subjective interpretations of the work world will be meaningless.

A final area not directly addressed in this volume also calls for further attention—namely, the decision-making process for entry into the labor market. Although opinions differ as to the precise time frame, researchers generally agree that in the period from preadolescence onward young people devote considerable effort to formulating an effective strategy for coping with the transition from school to work. Leontief and Duchin (1986) have predicted major transformations in the educational system and labor market in the next fifteen years. However, our limited understanding of the subjective underpinnings of the decision-making process prevents us from capitalizing on such projections, even though technological transformations are moving at a rapid pace, and our children and youth are actively engaged in or are monitoring these events.

The chapters in this sourcebook were brought together for one purpose: to present a critical mass of research on the subjective experiences of young people with regard to the adult work world. In so doing, we hope that additional research interest will be generated and that our understanding of the relatively invisible interchange that exists between our youth and the work world will become more apparent.

References

Garraty, J. A. *Unemployment in History*. New York: Harper & Row, 1978.

Leontief, W., and Duchin, F. *The Future Impact of Automation on Workers*. New York: Oxford University Press, 1986.

Reich, R. B. *The Next American Frontier*. New York: Times Books, 1983.

Youniss, J. E., and Smollar, J. *Adolescent Relations with Mothers, Fathers and Friends*. Chicago: University of Chicago Press, 1985.

John H. Lewko is associate professor of child development and director of the Centre for Research in Human Development, Laurentian University, Sudbury, Ontario, Canada.

Index

A

Adolescents: conclusions on, 89–91; decision making by, 90; developmental work perceptions of, 33–49; and economic conditions, 21–31; employment viewed by, 37–41; new technology viewed by, 51–67; parents' jobs viewed by, 3–19; relational-developmental view of, 34–35; unemployment viewed by, 41–46

Alberta, economic conditions study in, 22, 24

Albreton, Work and Family Life Project in, 75

Attitudes Toward the World of Work Index, 24, 25, 26, 27

B

Barke, C., 31
Becker, B. E., 26, 30
Best, F., 73, 86
Billig, M., 59, 66
Birnbaum, B., 73, 87
Blishen, B. R., 23, 30
Bloom-Feshbach, J., 1, 2, 22, 31
Bloom-Feshbach, S., 1, 2, 22, 31
Boxer, H., 3n
Breakwell, G. M., 1, 51, 52, 54, 55, 56, 59, 63, 66–67, 89, 90
Bronfenbrenner, U., 73, 86
Bryant, B. K., 80, 86
Burbank, M., 3n, 7, 19
Brulingham, D., 70, 86
Butler, D., 30, 31

C

Canada, economic studies in, 22–30
Career, comprehension of concept of, 38–40
Children: conclusions on, 89–91; and economic conditions, 21–31; and family economic environment, 69–87; parental jobs viewed by, 3–19; stress on, 69–70, 71–72; work-family conflicts viewed by, 13–16

Cobb, S., 72, 74, 86
Cochrane, R., 59, 66
Cognition, and work perception, 34–55, 46–48
Computers, and new technology, 63
Cooper, D., 69–70, 86
Cotgrove, S., 52, 55, 67
Crouter, A. C., 33, 48, 73, 86
Cummings, S., 3, 18

D

DeFleur, M. L., 3, 4, 18
Development, and work perception, 33–49
Duchin, F., 90, 91
Durrett, M. E., 3, 18
Dyer, W. G., 4, 13, 18

E

Economic uncertainty study: analysis of, 21–31; background on, 21–22; context for, 22–23; and direct or indirect exposure, 25–26; discussion of, 28–30; exposure variable in, 23–24; instruments in, 24–25; method of, 22–25; and negative or positive climate, 26–28; procedure for, 25; results from, 25–28; subjects for, 23. See also Family economic environment; Unemployment

Elder, G. H., 72, 74, 86
Employment: adolescent view of, 37–41; concepts in, 38–40; and worker qualities, 37–38

F

Family economic environment: analysis of, 69–87; background on, 69–70; case studies of, 80–85; conclusion on, 85–86; defining, 72–74; economic characteristics in, 76–80; fac-

Family economic environment *(continued)*
tors related to, 73–74; and job status, 72–73; measuring, 74; and parental unemployment, 70–71; study of, 75–85. *See also* Economic uncertainty study
Farran, D. C., 1, 69–70, 71, 86, 87, 89
Feather, N. T., 29, 31
Feinman, S., 70, 87
Ferber, M., 73, 87
Fife-Schaw, C., 1, 51, 52, 54, 55, 56, 63, 66–67, 89, 90
Fisher, L., 87
Freud, A., 70, 86
Furnham, A., 30, 31, 41, 43, 45, 48
Furth, H. G., 1, 28, 31, 33, 35–36, 46, 48, 49, 90

G

Garduque, L., 33, 49
Garraty, J. A., 89, 91
Garrett, J. B., 55, 60, 67
Germany, Federal Republic of, skilled labor in, 52
Glaser, R., 87
Glick, P. C., 71, 87
Goldberg, D., 57, 60, 67
Goldstein, B., 40, 48
Gornick, L., 14, 15, 18
Gortmaker, S. L., 72, 87
Grant Foundation, W. T., 3n
Greenberger, E., 1, 2, 33, 49

H

Haan, N. S., 47, 48
Hall, D. T., 38, 49
Hamilton, S. F., 33, 48
Heller, K. A., 1, 2, 22, 31
Hills, S. M., 26, 30
Hoyles, C., 63, 67

I

Intelligence, and new technology, 64
International Labor Organization of the United Nations, 51–52, 67

J

Jacobi, M., 33, 49
Jahoda, M., 38–39, 48
Japan, skilled labor in, 52

K

Kasl, S., 72, 74, 86
Katz, M. H., 3, 14, 18
Kiecolt-Glaser, J., 86, 87
Knowledge. *See* Occupational knowledge
Kohlberg, L., 35, 47, 48
Kohn, M. L., 3, 18
Kuhn, P., 47, 48
Kunin, T., 18

L

Langer, J., 47, 48
Leahy, R. L., 37, 43, 45, 48–49
Lee, T. R., 52, 54, 55, 56, 63, 66–67
Leontief, W., 90, 91
Lerner, R. M., 33, 49
Leverhulme Trust, 51n
Lewis, M., 70, 87
Lewko, J. H., 1, 2, 21, 26, 31, 89, 90, 91
Looft, W. R., 3, 18

M

Macleod, H., 63, 67
McLoughlin, Q., 14, 18
McRoberts, H. A., 23, 30
MacRury, K., 22, 24, 25, 28, 31
Maguire, T., 22, 24, 25, 28, 41
Mann, F. C., 14, 18
Margolis, L. H., 1, 69, 71, 87, 89
Marini, M. M., 39, 40, 49
Meacham, J. A., 34, 49
Medicaid, 73
Mills, S. C., 54, 67
Mirels, H. L., 55, 60, 67
Moscovici, S., 53, 67
Mott, P. E., 14, 18

N

Nelson, R. C., 3, 18
New technology: adolescent attitudes

to, 57–66; adult attitudes to, 54–55; analysis of attitudes to, 51–67; background on, 51–52; concepts of, 53–54, 65–66; conclusions on, 66; and consistency of attitudes, 58–59; and gender and training effects, 56; and implications for action, 62–65; motivation and views of, 65–66; and socioeconomic beliefs, 55; sources of motivation to, 59–62; structure of attitudes to, 57–58

North Carolina Work and Family Life Project, 74, 85

Nowak, T., 73, 87

O

Oakland, child development study in, 72

O'Brien, G. E., 29, 31

O'Bryant, S. L., 3, 18

Occupation, comprehension of concept of, 38–40

Occupational aspirations, and new technology, 63–64

Occupational knowledge: acquisition of, 3–4; accuracy of, 10–13; claimed, 9–10; sources of, 8–9

Ogrocki, P., 87

Ohlde, C., 31

Oldham, J., 40, 48

O'Neil, J. M., 21, 30, 31

Ontario, economic uncertainty study in, 2–30

P

Parental jobs study: and accuracy of knowledge, 10–13; analysis of, 3–19; background on, 3–5; and claimed knowledge, 9–10; and future research directions, 16–18; and job satisfaction, 11, 13; limitations of, 5; measures in, 6–7; procedures for, 5–7; results from, 8–16; sample characteristics in, 7–8; sampling for, 5–6; and sources of knowledge, 8–9; target population for, 5; and work-family conflicts, 13–16

Parents: job status of, 72–73; and new technology, 60–61; and work-family conflict, 15–16. See also Economic uncertainty study; Family economic environment

Patterson, G. R., 70–71, 87

Pautler, K. J., 1, 21, 26, 31, 71, 87, 90

Pearce, A., 53

Pennebaker, J. W., 3, 18

Piaget, J., 47, 49

Piggott, T., 31

Piotrkowski, C. S., 1, 3, 4, 7, 14, 15, 17, 18–19, 89

Pleck, J. H., 14, 15, 19

Protestant work ethic (PWE), and new technology, 55, 60, 61–62, 66

Q

Quinn, R. P., 73, 87

R

Reich, R. B., 29, 31, 89, 91

Robins, L., 70, 87

Romaniuk, E., 22, 24, 25, 28, 31

Rosenberg, M., 57, 67

Ross, L., 45, 49

Rutter, M., 69, 74, 87

S

Santilli, N. R., 1, 33, 34, 36, 49, 90

Schau, C. G., 48, 49

Select Panel for the Promotion of Child Health, 71, 87

Self-esteem, and new technology, 60, 61–62, 66

Siann, G., 63, 67

Siegel, S., 8, 19

Smith, R. S., 70, 87

Smollar, J., 34, 49, 90, 91

Snyder, K., 73, 87

Social referencing, 70

Socioeconomic Index for Canadian Occupations, 23

Special Supplemental Food Program for Women, Infants, and Children, 77

Spencer, J., 52, 54, 55, 56, 63, 67

Spreicher, C., 87

Staines, G. L., 14, 15, 19, 73, 87

Starfield, B., 72, 87

Stark, E., 1, 3, 7, 19, 89

Steinberg, L. G., 1, 2, 33, 49

Stout, J., 87
Strang, S., 3n
Stress: on children, 69–70, 71–72; from parental unemployment, 70–71
Super, D. E., 38, 49
Switzerland, skilled labor in, 52

T

Taebel, D., 3, 18
Technology. *See* New technology
Terry, S. L., 72, 87
Tittle, C. K., 4, 19
Tollefson, N., 31
Tremaine, L. S., 48, 49
Turkle, S., 63, 67

U

Unemployment: adolescent view of, 41–46; causes of, 41–43; effects of, 43–44; help for, 44; and logical reasoning, 47–48; society's view of, 45. *See also* Economic uncertainty study; Family economic environment
United Kingdom: childhood stress study in, 70; new technology study in, 53–66; skilled labor in, 52

V

Vondracek, F. W., 33, 49

W

Warwick, D. P., 14, 18
Watts, D., 31
Webley, P., 45, 49
Werner, E. E., 70, 87
Work: children's and adolescents' views of parental, 3–19; comprehension of concept of, 38–40; conclusions on, 89–91; and economic conditions, 21–31; ethic toward, 55, 60, 61–62, 66; and family conflicts, 13–16; and family economic environment, 69–87; and new technology, 51–67; perceptions of, 33–49
Work and Family Life (WFL) Project: case studies in, 80–85; conclusion on, 85–86; economic characteristics for, 76–80; introduced, 75–76; sample for, 75–76
Work perception: analysis of developmental approach to, 33–49; background on, 33–34; conclusion on, 48; discussion of, 40–41, 45–46; of employment, 37–41; and logical reasoning, 46–48; measuring, 36–37; relational-developmental view of, 34–36; study of, 36–48; of unemployment, 41–46
Wrigley, V., 45, 49

Y

Youniss, J. E., 34, 49, 90, 91